To Abraham,

Together we can truly make a different[ce]

[signature]

(Jan '09)

HONESTY WORKS!

HONESTY WORKS!

STEVEN GAFFNEY

*Real-World Solutions to
Common Problems at
Work and Home*

JMG Publishing

Honesty Works: Real-World Solutions to Common Problems at Work and Home
by Steven Gaffney

ISBN-13: 978-0-9715377-2-9
ISBN 10: 0-9715377-2-0

Published by JMG Publishing
Arlington, Virginia

This book is designed to provide accurate and authoritative information. All of the stories and anecdotes described in this book are based on true experiences, but most of the names are pseudonyms, and some situations have been changed slightly to protect each individual's privacy. It is sold with the understanding that neither the Author nor the Publisher is engaged in rendering counseling or other professional services by publishing this book. The Author and Publisher specifically disclaim any liability or loss that is incurred as a consequence, directly or indirectly, of the use and application of any of the contents of this book.

Interior design by Pneuma Books, LLC. For more info, visit www.pneumabooks.com
Cover photo by Clay & Company, Clay Blackmore
Cover design 2005 TLC Graphics, www.TLCGraphics.com

"There are two ways to live your life — one is as though nothing is a miracle, the other is as though everything is a miracle."
— Albert Einstein

*This book is dedicated to those who
choose to live their lives as though
everything is a miracle.*

*To all of my clients,
participants, family & friends —
together we can make a difference.*

Table of Contents

Acknowledgments

WITH A GREAT deal of concern about missing someone, I would like to thank the following people (not in any particular order) who have made a huge difference in the creation of this book. Thank you to:

Each of the participants in my keynote speeches and seminars for pushing me, encouraging me, and providing me with so many wonderful and insightful anecdotes and ideas.

My operations and business manager, Christina Taylor. Words cannot begin to describe how amazing she is. She makes everything happen behind the scenes, while doing the job of many. Running the company with her by my side makes anything possible.

My past client, now associate, and wonderful friend, Juanita Pappert. Juanita contributed to this book through her writing, editing, and her tireless commitment to provide access to this work.

One of my dearest friends, Theo Androus. Theo has served as my business coach and advisor and has contributed through his writing, editing, and comments.

My Mastermind Group for giving me great business wisdom — Bill Cates, who has been an amazing advisor to me over the years and Willie Jolley, who relentlessly encourages me to think huge!

My Extraordinary Results Team for providing the great advice, ideas, and techniques that compose so much of this book. Mike Casey, who is one of my best friends; Roger Johnson, who is such a wise man; Gary Helmenski, who was the first person that believed I could make it in this business; Howard Needham, who as the newest member has been an immediate support; and Peter Kelley, whose commitment to his son inspires me.

My parents, Marina and John Gaffney. Their love and commitment to me is breathtaking.

My nephews — Tom, Nicholas, and Matthew Vanderslice. They keep me grounded to what is truly important. They are a never-ending source of great material, smiles on my face, and love in my heart.

My sister, Lisa Gaffney. She is the mother of my three nephews and has always been there for me.

My brother, Andrew Gaffney. He was one family member who truly believed I could make it as a professional speaker and seminar leader.

My grandparents, Guilio and Marchella Oreffice and John and Mina Gaffney. Although they have passed away, their memory and influence are prevalent throughout this book.

My longtime friend, Tom Brouillette. I missed acknowledging him in my first book, *Just Be Honest*. He was my original mentor in honest communication and taught me how to get along with other people. I shudder to think where I would be without his amazing wisdom and friendship.

Jen Ellefson, who put together the original draft of this book.

Special thanks to all those who reviewed, advised, and helped us edit the draft of this book — John and Marina Gaffney, Keith and Karen Taylor, Bill Cates, Jennifer Covino, Lisa Gaffney, Dave Avrin, Jennifer Ellefson, and Kristin Arnold.

Also, special thanks to Dave Avrin at Avrin Public Relations for *enhancing* and ensuring that this book really makes a difference in the lives of many.

Introduction

DO YOU EVER wish people would keep their promises? Do you wish someone you live or work with was different? Do you want someone to take action? Are you tired of people complaining? Are you tired of your own complaints? Do you ever feel as if you are living out the same day with the same problems over and over again?

The key to resolving these issues is to be honest with yourself as well as with others. How can you do this effectively with long-term results? This book has the solutions.

Honesty Works: Real-World Solutions to Common Problems at Work and Home provides quick, realistic strategies and techniques to implement. Each solution is designed to stand alone and make an immediate difference at work and home, whether it is by enhancing honesty, turning around negativity, repairing a relationship, boosting your career, or running meetings quickly and effectively. You do not need to read this book all at once or

1

even in chapter order; you can pick and choose chapters to read and implement as needed.

You will notice a common theme throughout all of the strategies though. They are all honest, sincere, and they work. The problem with gimmicky strategies is that they may initially cause a change in your relationship with someone else. But once the other person catches on to the strategy, they may feel manipulated, and then the relationship may be damaged. Instead, by using these honest strategies that are in no way manipulative, you will see that honesty *does* work and will produce a dramatic difference in your life!

Honesty is the switch that can set your train on a different track. When a train switches tracks, the change is slight at first. But over time the change is dramatic. Introducing honesty into your relationships will lead you to a very different destination.

Furthermore, a change in one relationship can positively influence other areas and relationships. For example, fixing a relationship at work can affect your home life, while fixing a relationship at home can affect your work life. Every change has a ripple effect on the other relationships in your life.

For that reason alone, the principles established in this book can help you accomplish your dreams. The first step is to carefully consider the advice presented in this book. The second is to implement it and reap the benefits and rewards that unfold along the way.

The Basis of All Communication

HAVE YOU EVER encountered someone who used perfect body language and had impeccable pronunciation and grammar skills, yet you didn't believe a word they said? Conversely, have you ever encountered someone who stumbled and stammered, seemed nervous and lacked confidence, but still you believed them? How smooth you are does not matter, but sincerity does.

How do you feel when you encounter someone who is trying to emulate someone else and consequently appears artificial? Imagine John F. Kennedy talking like Mahatma Gandhi or Ronald Reagan emulating Martin Luther King, Jr. The notion is silly, yet all of these people are thought of as master communicators. Although each of them had their own style, their sincerity and passion made them dynamic speakers.

Body language, word choice, tone, and inflection are important as well, but nothing is as important as sincerity. Why? Because our true thoughts and feelings are conveyed in every aspect of our interactions.

Remember, most of us are lousy actors and actresses. People can detect when we are being sincere — when the inside matches the outside. Ralph Waldo Emerson said, "What you do speaks so loud that I cannot hear what you say." Your deeds should match your words. You do not have to be perfect, but you do have to be *perfectly yourself*.

Uncover the Hidden Cost
of an Unresolved Issue

HAVE YOU EVER had an issue or problem with someone that just didn't seem worth resolving? Many people rationalize issues or problems by saying: "It's no big deal," or "I can handle it," or "It's not worth bringing up." We often believe that the cost of bringing up an issue is greater than not bringing it up. But is that really the case?

Studies have revealed the following statistics: 80 percent of work problems are due to a lack of open communication; up to 75 percent of employees leave their jobs due to communication issues; and communication issues cause every employee to lose seven weeks per year of productivity. These are alarming statistics.

Consider this: if you live a normal life under normal circumstances, you will probably spend more time at work than at any other activity in your life — other than sleeping. This means that you'll spend more time working than with loved ones, participating in your favorite hobbies, or pursuing your favorite activities.

For that reason, I find it amazing how many people have issues at work and rationalize by telling themselves *it's just work*. Another common rationalization is that we work so that we can enjoy our personal lives. The trouble with that is that we often pay a steep price for not confronting issues — the price of not enjoying work, among other things.

There are certainly times to let small or unimportant things go, but don't lie to yourself about which issues are the ones you really need to handle. Don't let issues go unresolved and suffer the consequences. *You* must make the decision whether or not to bring up an issue; just make sure you are aware of the steep price of ignoring it — including the hidden, intangible costs — so you can determine what to do. How can you do that? Take the Honest Communication Cost Questionnaire, in which the unresolved issue/problem/person/situation is called X.

HONEST COMMUNICATION COST QUESTIONNAIRE

Note: Although this questionnaire focuses on work issues, you can easily adapt it to personal and home issues as well.

Time

How much time do you spend per day thinking about X? Please include the time you spend thinking about whether you *should* deal with X and *how* you might deal with X. Please estimate the total time per day — 15 minutes, 30 minutes, 1 hour, 2 hours, and so on.

How much time do you spend per day on the ripple effect — that is the extra time it takes to do other tasks because you are so preoccupied with X? Please include the time you re-read documents and re-write reports. And what about the effect of missing what people are saying about other projects, so it takes you longer to do those projects? Estimate that time as well. Estimate the total time per day — 15 minutes, 30 minutes, 1 hour, 2 hours, and so on.

How much time do you spend trying to work around X? Please include the extra time you spend in meetings and conversations because you don't have the right information or because the real issue isn't being discussed. Also include the time your extra effort takes to try to get the required information. Estimate the total time per day — 15 minutes, 30 minutes, 1 hour, 2 hours, and so on.

What is the total amount of time per day? _____

Now multiply the total by the days in a week and multiply that total by the weeks in a year. What is the grand total of time per year? _____

Just 30 minutes a day, multiplied by 5 (for the number of work days in a week), multiplied by 48 weeks in a year (accounting for vacation, holidays, and sick leave) equals 120 hours, or 15 days (figuring 8-hour work days). That equals 3 work weeks! An hour a day comes out to 6 weeks or 1 ½ months! Couldn't you use that extra time?

The one commodity that we can never get back in life is time.

What is this wasted time worth to you? Based on your lost time, do you think it's time to take care of X?

Confidence and Motivation

List the projects, goals, or opportunities that X is stopping you from doing. Please include any hobbies, dreams, wishes, and relationships that you are not pursuing or at least not pursuing with the commitment, enthusiasm, and zest that you could.

List other issues you are not tackling because of your lost confidence from not taking care of X. Please include other issues with that same person or issues with other people that you are too intimidated, scared, upset, or demoralized to handle — all because you know you haven't even taken care of X.

Are these issues, relationships, projects, goals, opportunities, and dreams worth sacrificing? One of the saddest phrases is someone saying, "I wonder how my life would have been different if I would have..." When you are ninety years old and you look back at this time, will you regret not resolving X?

Relationships

List the other relationships in your life that are suffering because of your failure to handle X. Think about who you have been impatient, short-tempered, or annoyed with because X remains unresolved. If X is work-related, what relationships at home are paying the price? If X is a personal issue, think about what relationships at work are paying the price. Please list all the relationships that are suffering.

What relationships do you have that feel disconnected because of X? Think about people you are not connecting with or are not close to because of your preoccupation with X. Please list all those relationships.

Are these suffering and disconnected relationships worth the price of not resolving X? You might think you can handle it, and maybe you can. But can others? Consider the price of divorce, being fired, or finding out your child is in trouble because of your failure to resolve X. Maybe your relationships are fine now, or perhaps they are limping along, but what price will you and others pay in the future? Is this price acceptable, or is it time to take care of X?

Teamwork

How is X affecting how people are working together? On a scale of 1 to 10, how effective is your team now because of X? If X were to be resolved, where would your team be? Please consider turnover and lost productivity among other things.

How many people have you lost from the team? Remember, up to 75 percent of people leave their jobs because of communication issues. People frequently say they are leaving because of money, but they often don't state the real reason for fear of burning their bridges. Estimate how many people have left your organization. Multiply the number of people by two times the amount of each of their salaries, since it takes between two to three times someone's salary to find a suitable replacement, train them, and get them to the same level.

Is this level of efficiency acceptable to you? What about the wasted money? Is it acceptable to others? Is there a storm brewing on your team that could blow any time? Could that storm lead to missed opportunities, failure to get promoted, missed goals, or the departure of other team members? Can you live with the true costs of not dealing with X? Is it time to address X?

Stress and Quality of Life

On a scale of 1 to 10 (1 feeling awful, 10 feeling great), how happy and joyful are you now? If X was resolved, what would your level of happiness and enjoyment be?

How many stressful days per week do you have over X? Please consider how many days you feel drained, sad, or experience a lack of energy. Multiply the number of days per week by the appropriate number of weeks in the year. (See the example in the Time section.)

How many nights per week have you lost sleep because of your preoccupation with X? Multiply the number of nights per week by the appropriate number of weeks in the year. Also consider the effect of lost sleep on your productivity the following day.

Is this level of happiness and enjoyment okay with you? Are the stressful days, sleepless nights, and lost productivity worth it? Are you rationalizing that it will get better soon? How long have you been saying that? Do a gut check. Can you pay this price, or is it time to take care of X?

The Total Cost

Look at the big picture: the lost time; lost confidence and motivation; the missed projects, goals, dreams, and opportunities; the damage to your other relationships; the cost in teamwork and effectiveness; and the lack of joy and your quality of life. Each category of costs affects the other. Is this price worth paying? You are the one who must decide.

Remember, the costs will only grow if the problems are left unattended. As someone once said, "Problems are not like wine; they do not get better over time." The truth is, problems get worse, and they have a ripple effect on other situations and relationships.

The risk of resolving an issue is minimal when compared to the enormous and mounting costs of not resolving it. Think about how wonderful it feels to resolve an issue, which in turn affects every other dimension of your life.

Wouldn't it be great if that weight was lifted off of your shoulders? Now you are aware of the real costs. The question is, what do you want to do about it? Seize the moment, stop the pain, and take action! The clock is ticking... (See "The Worst Lies" in real-world solution 8.)

Eliminate Painful Meetings

I REMEMBER BEING interviewed by a writer for an article about effective meetings that was to appear in a national magazine. The writer began the interview by saying, "I don't want any of the old standard tips; I want new tips."

I replied, "Well, people wouldn't need new tips if they used the old tips." This isn't what the writer wanted to hear, nor is this what many of us want to hear, but this is the truth. If we used what we already know, we could avoid a lot of problems — including unproductive meetings.

Have you ever sat through a meeting only to realize that the real issues were being discussed *outside* the meeting? Have you ever attended a meeting and asked yourself what the point was?

Many organizations experience what I like to call the *soap opera effect* — you go to one meeting, then miss a few meetings, and then when you go to the next meeting, it is as if you never missed any meetings at all! Just like the afternoon soaps, you only have to check in once in a while to get caught up.

If everyone was more upfront and honest, meetings could be a wonderful vehicle to accomplish our objectives and goals. It's staggering to think of the time, productivity, and money lost due to unproductive meetings. It doesn't have to be that way.

Here are twelve simple, honest tips for running results-producing meetings in a fraction of the time your unproductive meetings take. If these tips seem like common sense, then ask yourself if people are actually using them. The more tips you use, the more effective your meetings will be.

1. **Only include the people who need to attend.**
   If you are worried about insulting someone who is not included, ask them if they really want to be included. Most likely, people will be thankful that they don't have to attend another meeting and can get the information they need through other means, such as the meeting minutes.

2. **Make sure attendees understand the benefit of attending.**
   If you are having problems with attendance at meetings, it is usually a sign that people do not see the benefit of being there, but they may not be upfront about this. Instead they may say, "I got caught up with things," or "I was too busy." Of course, if they received a million dollars for attending, they would have found a way. It is often a question of motivation. Here are four questions to ask yourself before calling a meeting: Do we really need to have this meeting? Could we accomplish the same results in another, less time-consuming way? If not, what benefit does the meeting give the attendees? How am I going to convince them of this benefit? The answers to these questions will

help you determine what to do to increase the attendance and effectiveness of your meeting.

3. **Start the meeting on time.**
   How often have you intentionally arrived late to a meeting, because you knew you wouldn't miss anything anyway? Many of us are conditioned to understand that meetings never start on time. It doesn't have to be that way. Start the meeting at the designated time, continue through the agenda, and don't provide any reiteration for the latecomers. If anyone requests a review of the missed information, decline. This action will train the attendees that it is important to be on time.

4. **Clearly define the purpose of the meeting.**
   At the start of each meeting, clearly state the meeting's purpose. Also, make sure the purpose is written on the agenda. When deciding on the meeting's purpose, think in terms of the overall result or outcome you want to produce. When the purpose is stated upfront, it is easier to re-direct those who would take the meeting off track. If someone brings up an issue that is off topic, simply say, "Since the purpose of this meeting is [fill in the blank], can we tackle that issue at the next meeting, when we could allow time for it?"

5. **Have a written agenda.**
   I find it amazing how often meetings are run without an agenda. If you don't have a map of where you're going, you're certain to get sidetracked or lost. Even if it is an impromptu or emergency meeting, you can write out a basic agenda on a flip chart or a white board. The point is to have some kind of written agenda clearly visible to everyone so the meeting can stay on track.

6. **Prioritize the agenda.**

This may seem obvious, but how many meetings have you been to in which the most inconsequential matters were discussed at the beginning of the meeting, while the important items got pushed back until half the room had either become disinterested, fallen asleep, or slipped out? By prioritizing an agenda, you ensure that the most important things will be accomplished first. This is also an incentive for people to show up on time, because they know the important items will be discussed first.

7. **Specify a time frame for each agenda issue.**

This enables you to manage the individual portions of a meeting, so you can accomplish everything you intend to. It also gives you another tool for reducing excessive elaboration or off-point discussions. If these discussions occur, you can say, "I am sorry, but as you can see, we are running short on the allotted time we have for this particular agenda item. So, in order to prevent this meeting from running over, we will need to move on. Please see me afterward if we need to discuss this issue further."

8. **Begin with a quick review of what happened at the last meeting and who agreed to do what.**

Review the last meeting's action items. Go around the room to get updates on what everyone had agreed to accomplish by this meeting (see tip 10). This clearly sends the message that you expect the participants to do what they said they would do. It also helps ensure accountability and prevents the soap opera effect.

9. **Bring up any "elephant in the room" conversations.**

   The tension in some meetings can be thick enough to cut with a knife. Sometimes, people ignore issues, because they fear that bringing it up will have a negative effect on the meeting. However, failing to mention an issue can make the meeting leader appear weak. Furthermore, neglecting the issue leaves the door open for someone else to bring it up at a less opportune time. Proactively address uncomfortable issues early in the meeting and then move on.

10. **Make sure you end the meeting with action items.**

    Specify who is going to do what and in what time frame. You can summarize it, or you can go around the room and let each person summarize what they are going to do by what date. This helps ensure that participants take ownership and are clear on what they are going to do. Make sure the action items have a specific time frame written down in the meeting minutes These minutes should be circulated after the meeting for clarity and accountability. Then, as stated in tip 8, review this list at the beginning of the next meeting.

11. **Conclude with a compliment and/or acknowledgement.**

    End things on a good note, even if it was a tough meeting. For example, you could say, "Thanks for taking the time to be here. I specifically want to acknowledge those of you who shared your thoughts and ideas. It allowed us to handle important issues in the meeting in an upfront manner." The more specific the acknowledgement and praise, the better.

12. **End the meeting on time.**

    When a meeting extends past the time limit, attendees become resentful and stop participating, simply because they want the meeting to end. Some will go as far as withholding important information or not bringing up an important issue because they do not want to prolong the meeting. This delay could also cause a chain reaction on your attendees' schedules for the remainder of the day. What can you do to avoid this? End on time. If everything was not covered, you can arrange to cover those items in another setting or at another time. If you must exceed the time limit, always seek approval from everyone in attendance. Give everyone a new, specific time for the meeting to end. Even if you are the boss, acknowledge and seek approval to go over the time limit. It sends a message that you care and respect attendees' time. This is a more effective approach than the standard, "I need just a few more minutes." When most of us hear this, we think, *we'll be in here forever.*

If you use these twelve tips, many problems that ordinarily arise in meetings will simply never come up. You don't need to use all, or even most, of the ideas outlined here to appropriately and effectively manage group dynamics in a meeting or during a presentation. However, by using as many as you can, your meetings and presentations will produce results and achieve the goals you want — and your attendees will probably thank you for it. (See "7 Benefits that Drive Human Behavior" in real-world solution 4.)

7 Benefits That Drive Human Behavior

WHETHER YOU WANT to obtain new business, sell your boss on an idea, or even if you want something from your family and friends, remember the universal language we all speak — what's in it for me?

This may seem like common sense, but it is usually what is missing when we make requests. When someone asks us to do something, we tend to evaluate it and consider the request based on what is in it for us. When we ask someone else to do something, we usually think about what is in it — for us. Therein lies the problem. We think about what is in it for us — even though the key to getting the things we want is to be honest and upfront about what is in it for the other person.

Want a raise? Think about what's in it for your boss. Want someone to assist you on a project? Think about what's in it for them. Want someone to turn in some paperwork on time, turn in a time sheet on time, or come to a meeting on time? You know what to do. The truth is that people will go to great lengths, overcome huge obstacles, or carve out time in a very busy day if there is enough benefit for them to do so.

Children are great models of this behavior. Without any training, children realize that to get what they want, they have to explain how others will benefit. Notice what children will say when they are being persuasive: "I will love you more," "I will clean up my room," "I will stop bugging you," and my all-time favorite, "I won't ever ask you for anything else." Like children, we need to state the benefit to the other person upfront and clearly.

So, when you are thinking about asking someone to do something, whether in your business or personal life, think about what would persuade them to agree and be honest upfront with them. Think about and implement MT. SAMIE.

MT. SAMIE

The acronym MT. SAMIE stands for the seven major benefits that drive human behavior. The key to cooperation is to connect your requests to some of these benefits. The more benefits, the more likely the other person will agree and fulfill your request.

1. **Money.**

   Money clearly motivates people. If you can show those who are motivated by money how fulfilling your request will help them make or save money, you will probably capture their attention. For many organizations, money/revenue is a primary motivator. As an employee, if you can show how your request will make or save the organization more money, you may motivate the powers that be to take action.

2. **Time.**

It is staggering how many people are time-impoverished. If you can show how fulfilling your request will save the other person time, you may motivate the person to take action. For example, you might say, "Boss, can you help me handle Herman? I figure this situation with him is wasting about 20 percent of my time. So if you could help me handle Herman better, I could save all that time, which would enable me to take things off your plate and save you time." The benefit for the boss in that situation is clear.

3. **Security.**

People tend to search for things that will give them a sense of security and help them avoid risk. Look at what people will put up with in an effort to stay where they are in a job or in a relationship that is not really what they want. Why? Because they are afraid of risk, and they like the security. A leader can capitalize on people's desire for security by reminding his or her staff that the best way to protect against reorganization is for everyone to do the best job they can. A manager can tell his or her employees that they need to complete a task because it is part of their jobs, and they will be held account-able. The approach may seem heavy-handed, but if someone is not doing the job, a manager sometimes needs to be just that. This is, hopefully, a situation of last resort.

4. **Achievement.**

Achievement is about producing results. Have you ever done something that was not on your to-do list and then written it in just to have the satisfaction of crossing it off? We like the feeling of accomplishing things; we like achieving goals. If your request will help someone achieve something they want to achieve, they'll likely do what you want. A leader who clearly shows how the organization's vision and goals will benefit every employee understands this. The key is not to *say* everyone will benefit but to show people exactly *how*. On the flipside, employees whose requests would help the boss achieve his or her goals are more likely to get attention.

5. **Making a difference.**

Making a difference is one of the top motivators for people. We all want to make a difference, a *real* difference. How often have you stayed at work extra hours just to help someone out, whether or not you made any money from it? How often do you donate your time for community service? How about doing big favors or something really nice for someone? We do this because we want to contribute. Making a difference for others makes us feel good. Now, oddly enough, we sometimes use this benefit against ourselves. How? When we hide how important something is to us or the effect it has on us, we motivate the other person to continue their actions, because they are unaware of our feelings and the effect of their actions. People will often stop doing what they are doing if we simply let them know how their actions are affecting us. You might be surprised how often people have no idea about the effect of their actions. Consider yourself for a moment. Has anyone ever gotten upset with you out of the blue over something you had been doing for a long time, but they had never told you how much it bothered them? What was your response? Probably, "Why didn't you say this before?" Think how many times you've heard someone — or yourself — say, "Well, if I'd only known how important it was to you..." Someone who is missing deadlines might stop missing them if we explain the effect it is having on us. The point here is that many people would help us if we would just ask and let them know what a difference it would make. This works on the personal side as well. Ask your significant other to make dinner or take out the garbage. Let them know what a difference it would make. It works a lot better than blaming.

6. **Image.**

Image is an interesting benefit, because people lie about caring. People say they don't care what others think about them, but truthfully most of us at least care about what some people think. For example, why do we have a hard time saying no to someone, even if we're already overcommitted? Because often we're concerned about how people will view us. And, incidentally, you *should* care about your image. For instance, suppose you work hard, but your boss perceives you as a person who does not work hard. Who has a problem? This is why organizations are so concerned, and rightfully so, with their images. For example, if there is a co-worker you have had some challenging conversations with, you might say, "My request is X. I have heard others comment on how much we are arguing, which is probably negatively affecting how both of us are perceived. Can we figure out some ways to work more effectively together?"

7. **Enjoyment.**

Many times we forget that enjoyment is a driving factor. If your request is going to increase someone's enjoyment, you're likely to capture their attention and increase their drive to resolve the issue. For example, someone who we find stressful and difficult to talk to is probably thinking the same thing about us. Use increased enjoyment and less stress as a benefit to resolve an issue. For example, suppose you have to talk to an employee about poor job performance. You could say, "Let's figure out a plan to get you back on track and then we won't have to have these stressful, upsetting conversations." By the way, children are experts at this one. They never forget to let us know that the benefit of giving them what they want is that they will stop annoying us and that things will be more peaceful and enjoyable for you.

The seven benefits of the acronym MT. SAMIE are not about manipulating the other person. The benefits are actually about respecting the other person. Rather than complaining because someone is not cooperating with you, agreeing with you, or giving you what you want, think and talk with that person to find out what might be in it for them. If you are not sure, you can always ask.

Even if your request is denied, by clearly mentioning what might be in it for them, you send a message that you are trying to consider their interests. Some of this may seem obvious — but obvious doesn't mean people are doing it. After all, when was the last time someone made a request of you and told you what would be in it for you? Speak the universal language of benefits. It is the key to getting what you want!

Effectively Deliver Bad News

SHARING BAD NEWS and difficult information is part of everyday life. The key is to proactively share such information before the other party discovers it. In the end, people usually find out the truth. Therefore, honest communication is critical to establishing credibility and trust, which in turn affects teamwork, productivity, profitability, and long-term success. Honest communication is the way we gain and keep the trust of our customers, potential clients, co-workers, and staff, as well as our family and friends. You can tell how open and trustworthy a relationship is by how willing someone is to share things that are difficult but important to hear.

When it's time to share bad news and difficult information, keep in mind three excuses to avoid and four techniques for effectively delivering the message.

THREE EXCUSES TO AVOID

1. **"It was not my job."**
   That rationale may seem okay, but it usually upsets the other person and makes you look like you are not a team player. After all, even if it was not your job, couldn't you have taken action and done something to help? History is filled with successful people who seized the moment and took charge.

2. **"No one told me."**
   If this is the case, the question to ask is, "Why?" Did you create an environment in which people are afraid to tell you difficult information?

3. **"Everyone agreed with me."**
   Just because everyone agreed with you does not let you off the hook for the outcome. After all, we tend to surround ourselves with people who think like us. Also, psychologists who study group dynamics report that people who don't think like the group tend to be alienated, left out, or even fired from their jobs. Just because everyone agrees with you does not mean you were right. In the 1400s, people thought the world was flat, but their collective thoughts didn't make it so.

FOUR TECHNIQUES FOR EFFECTIVELY DELIVERING THE MESSAGE

1. **Deliver it immediately.**
   Bad news about us is better coming from our own mouths than from someone else's. If someone else discovers our bad news before we divulge it, it undermines their trust in us, and they may begin to wonder what else we're hiding.

2. **Take 100 percent responsibility for your actions.**

   Remember, no one makes us do anything. We choose our actions for a variety of reasons. Great leaders and great coaches take responsibility for their *team's* actions as well as their own. When they take such responsibility, their fans usually receive any news favorably. Despite Ronald Reagan's popularity as president, he started slipping in the polls during the Iran-Contra affair until he took full responsibility for what transpired. Once he took responsibility, his popularity rose again.

3. **Get ahead of the curve on bad information.**

   If the future looks bleak or more bad information is possible, find out as much as you can and share it as quickly as possible before someone else discovers it. Years ago, tainted Tylenol killed people, yet the company survived the crisis in part because company officials quickly and openly shared what they knew with the public.

4. **Take immediate and widespread action to correct the situation.**

   This will help prevent erosion of trust, because people will feel more secure when they hear and witness that someone is doing something about the situation. Unfortunately, organizations often take a reactive wait-and-see approach — only to have the situation worsen. One organization I worked with waited to take care of their financial woes until they were forced to proceed with massive layoffs. The employees who remained became skeptical and lost trust that the situation would be reversed, so they started to seek employment elsewhere. How we respond to mistakes defines us. Consider the Tylenol example again. The company immediately pulled all the potentially deadly products off store shelves. They did not wait to be forced to take action; they proactively told the public what their company was doing to correct the situation and prevent further accidents.

No one likes to share bad information, but doing so honestly is imperative to maintaining the bond of trust. Trust is the foundation of all relationships, and honest communication is the key to developing and building the relationships we desire. (See "Ownership Attitude" in real-world solution 26 and "5 Keys to Effectively Sharing Your Viewpoint" in real-world solution 19.)

Eliminate Complaining

HAVE YOU HEARD someone complain about the same thing so often that you can predict exactly what they are going to say? It may seem as if they would rather complain than find a solution. That may be true for some, but many complainers really *do* want to resolve their complaint. They are simply stuck in the rut of complaining, and they don't know how to get out. To make matters more complex, sometimes the item being complained about is not really the issue.

Let's look at a few examples. Someone who complains about traffic may really want flexible work hours or the opportunity to telecommute. Someone who complains about his or her bills may really want a raise. The bottom line is this — we don't necessarily know what people want when they complain. We are not mind readers, and if we have to guess, then the *real* problems may go unresolved.

The following is a three-step process for resolving complaints. (You can also use this process to facilitate a meeting between people that are complaining and upset with each other.) Try The Complaint Ending Process™.

1. **Listen and acknowledge the emotions involved.**

   When people complain, they want to make sure they are heard. Until then, they won't be ready to resolve their issue. When someone complains, we must let them know that we *are* listening to them. One of the best ways to do this is to reflect and acknowledge the emotion you are hearing from them. You can acknowledge their emotions by saying something like, "I understand you are upset/stressed/annoyed." By acknowledging the emotions involved, you are more likely to help them diffuse and dissipate.

2. **Facilitate a possible solution.**

   Change the focus of the conversation from the complaint to a possible solution. You can do this by asking questions like: "What do you think we should do about it?" or "What would you like done about this?" or "How can we resolve this?" By asking solution-oriented questions, the complainer can often come up with great solutions. This is because they are the ones closest to the problem, and they often know how to fix it. Another positive result of this approach is that if the complainer discovers the solution, they are more likely to feel empowered. Now they have a vested interest in implementing the solution and seeing it to a successful conclusion. This is not to say we should never offer our advice. Instead wait and listen until you are sure you know what it is they really want and that they do in fact want our help. If the person does not want you to help fix the problem, and you ask them a facilitating, solution-oriented question such as, "What would you suggest," they will usually reply that they just wanted someone to listen. In that case, do just that and drop the issue.

3. **Be honest and work out an agreeable action plan.**
   If you are not able to give the complainer what they want, say so, and explain why you cannot. An explanation is very important. This way, the person at least understands and feels respected (even if they don't like our answer). Then follow up with, "What else would you suggest?" By doing this, you let them know that you can't always give them what they want, but you will be honest and will remain open to discussing other solutions. If they ask you for your ideas, feel free to tell them. The difference now is that they are asking for help rather than receiving unsolicited advice. Work together to come up with a solution that is agreeable to both of you.

Let's consider an example. An employee had been complaining for months about not having enough resources to do their job effectively. The boss focused all of her energy on suggesting ways for the employee to utilize the existing resources more effectively. However, the employee continued to complain. This not only began to annoy the boss, it soon began to irritate the entire team. Everyone was affected by the complaining.

Using the three steps, the boss produced some great results. The boss met with the employee privately and recounted the employee's complaints from the previous months. The boss said, "It seems as though you are upset and stressed." (This is acknowledging the emotions involved.) "What do you think we can do about the situation?" (This is brainstorming possible solutions.)

The employee stopped complaining, calmed down, and after a moment said, "I know we are understaffed. I have been working late, and I just want to be acknowledged for the extra time and energy I have been putting in, considering the lack of resources. And, of course, I hope that when things change, I will be considered for a promotion."

The lack of resources wasn't the real issue. The real issue was not feeling appreciated for the extra work done and the employee's desire to be promoted. The boss apologized and shared how much she appreciated the employee. Then they had a conversation about career possibilities for the employee.

Using The Complaint Ending Process™ won't resolve all the complaining that you encounter on a daily basis, but it should help significantly. And better yet, everyone will benefit from the improvement.

Stop E-mail Abuse

E-MAIL CAN BE a terrific, quick, and efficient form of communication, or it can be horrific. It all depends on how it is used. When people use e-mail in ways that are not effective, the results can be disastrous, costing organizations millions in lost productivity. Miscommunication and misinterpretations can easily occur with each click of the *send* button.

Have you been party to an e-mail war? How often are you *cc*'d on e-mails that you don't need to read (which only fill up your inbox, causing you to miss other vital messages)? These things can kill job satisfaction and overall daily effectiveness of individuals and their organizations.

Let's take a closer look at several e-mail problems and some possible solutions.

E-MAIL PROBLEMS

1. **E-mail is limited to one dimension of communication: the written word.**
   E-mail lacks the clarity of other forms of communication — namely, face-to-face communication. We cannot see facial expressions, notice body language, or hear tone of voice. So, when someone receives an e-mail, they imagine those things. If the e-mail recipient has issues with us, they will imagine the worst, no matter what our intentions were.

2. **You can't adjust an e-mail.**
   E-mail is a one-way conversation. During a conversation, we tend to make mid-course adjustments to adapt to the other person's reaction. We are unable to do this when we communicate through e-mail.

3. **You cannot control when an e-mail is read.**
   Have you ever had an e-mail upset you, only to read the same e-mail later in the day and discover that it's not upsetting after all? Our moods and emotions affect the way we read things. When we send an e-mail, we don't know what the recipient's mood will be when they read it. However, if we call or visit the person, we can back off and schedule a different time to discuss an issue if we see that it's not a good time. With e-mail, you have no control after you hit the send button.

4. **People interpret e-mails differently based on who the sender is.**
   If you are having challenges with someone, that person may misinterpret what you are saying, no matter how accurately you wrote the e-mail.

5. **E-mail can be manipulated.**
   E-mail can be saved, forwarded, circulated (to people you did not intend), and used against you. We have all written things we wish we hadn't. You can't do anything about the past, but you can do something about the present, which will affect your future.

6. **E-mail may get lost.**
   You can't necessarily assume an e-mail was received. For all sorts of weird and sometimes unknown reasons, e-mails can get lost in cyberspace.

E-MAIL SOLUTIONS

1. **Use e-mail for its four main purposes: to communicate information, to receive information, as a form of documentation, and for friendly correspondence.**
   For example, use e-mail to keep everyone informed of a project's status, to verify what was discussed in a face-to-face or phone conversation, to ask a quick question, to say hello, and to compliment.

2. **Do not use e-mail to resolve emotional upsets.**
   In other words, if you are upset with someone or someone is upset with you, do not use e-mail. Call the person or go talk to the person face to face. Given the inherent difficulties with communication via e-mail, it is not a good way to communicate emotions or resolve difficulties.

3. **State the purpose of your e-mail immediately.**
   By stating the purpose in the subject heading or in the first sentence of your text, you minimize the possibility that the

recipient will misinterpret your message or delete it before it
is read.

4. **Write e-mail as you would a newspaper article.**
   The first paragraph should contain the most pertinent information, with details following in subsequent paragraphs.
   People are busy and need the highlights. They may never finish the e-mail and may miss important information if it is
   buried in the body of the text. If appropriate, have a quick
   summary sentence at the end.

5. **If an e-mail volleys more than twice, pick up the phone.**
   If you e-mail back and forth with someone more than two
   times about the same issue, it is time to pick up the phone
   and get clarification. When e-mails volley back and forth
   about the same issue, it is often a sign that something else is
   going on (someone is really upset, doesn't understand, is
   being resistant, and so on).

6. **If you wouldn't want an e-mail published in a newspaper,
   don't send it.**
   You never know what will happen with your e-mail or to
   whom it will be forwarded once you press send.

Remember, e-mail can be either a terrific or horrific tool. It all
depends on how it is used. Be careful!

The Worst Lies

HOW OFTEN HAVE you said to yourself that you were going to start a new, healthy habit; a new routine; or something good for you; and then didn't do it? How about starting a diet, beginning a new exercise program, or quitting smoking? Has your inability to follow through reached the point that when you decide to do something, a little voice in your head chides, "Are you kidding? You've never stuck to it before! You'll never do it!" When this happens, you have told the worst lies you can tell: the lies you tell yourself. Now you no longer believe yourself.

Lies to ourselves undermine our own confidence to address issues, accomplish goals, and bring about necessary changes in our lives. They also undermine others' confidence in us, because they have witnessed the false proclamations and undelivered promises.

It doesn't have to be this way.

You can stop telling the worst lies of all by following these three simple steps:

1. **Be honest and declare that you will change.**
   The ability to change always starts within ourselves. If you find yourself trapped in the worst lies of all, let the people around you know that you are aware of your past undelivered promises. Others are often hesitant to bring up the subject because it could be embarrassing or humiliating. *You* bring it up. *You* mention it. Let them know that from this point forward, you will not say things you do not really mean.

2. **Give the people around you permission to challenge you if they see you going back to your old ways.**
   This is especially important when the same people have paid the price for your bad habits and undelivered promises over and over again.

3. **Decide on some consequences in advance if things don't change.**
   Let people know how serious you are about change by being ready to self-impose some consequences if things continue as they have in the past. You can even ask others to participate in the consequence. For example, if you have a track record of turning in late reports or being tardy to meetings, promise your co-worker that you will pay five dollars for every five minutes you are late. Or, perhaps you've committed to quit smoking. If so, you could put five dollars in a jar every time you have a cigarette. I know a group of co-workers who did this and then donated the money to charity. Or, if you have often promised your spouse that you will be home at night

by a certain time and you haven't kept your word, tell your spouse that you will treat him or her to a dinner of their choice every time you are late. Another option if you really feel brave, is to commit that for every failure, you will grant them one wish. A word of caution is needed here: only commit to a consequence you are willing to submit to. Otherwise you will compound the original problem of broken promises. This is not about the consequence. It is about ending the lies we tell and restoring our confidence in ourselves and the confidence of others in us.

The point is to believe what we say. The result will be soaring confidence, which will lead to accomplishing more than we ever thought possible. And at that point when you make a promise, the little voice inside your head will say, "Consider it done!"

How to Confront Liars

HAVE YOU EVER had the feeling someone was lying to you? Or not being *entirely* truthful? Worse yet, have you found yourself afraid to confront that person for fear of negative repercussions?

The Columbo Method is a simple and ingenious way to handle this potentially precarious problem. Remember the television show *Columbo*, starring Peter Falk? The fictional Columbo was a detective who solved murder mysteries. He was a humble and unassuming character who had the ability to get anyone to tell him anything, despite their initial resistance. When someone said something to Columbo that was conflicting or inconsistent, he would rub his head and say, "I noticed yesterday you said one thing, and now you are saying something else. I'm confused." He would say things like, "Could you clarify this?" or "Help me understand." Columbo did not accuse those he was questioning. By taking the responsibility for his confusion, he disarmed the other person — who then would slowly feel comfortable telling him the things he needed to know to solve the crime. The Columbo Method is to present the facts that appear to conflict, give the person the benefit of the doubt, and then ask questions for clarification.

In a business situation, Columbo might say, "I noticed you said you wanted the report right away, but I haven't heard from you since I gave you the report. Is everything okay?" Or, "Is there something else I can provide you with?"

By choosing not to blame or accuse the other person, we reduce the likelihood that they will be defensive or resistant and in turn increase the probability that they will reveal what is truly going on. Like a mystery, remember that things are not always as they appear. What may appear to be a lie may not be.

For example, suppose you asked a co-worker to help you with a project at 12 P.M., but he declined because of a conflicting meeting. Then you saw him leave the building at 12:00 P.M. Does this mean he was lying? Of course not. Perhaps his meeting was moved off-site, cancelled, or delayed. Perhaps he simply forgot about helping you. Perhaps he had a family emergency. There are a hundred reasons why he could have been leaving the building at 12:00 P.M.

There is a possibility that he *did* have a meeting when you talked that morning, but things later changed. The bottom line is that we just don't know the real reason until we ask. And this is where the Columbo Method can be used. You might say, "You told me you could not help on this project because you had a meeting, but then I noticed you left. I am confused. Is everything okay?" Or, "Am I missing something?"

The key to the Columbo Method is to remember that all you really know is that the facts are conflicting. You don't know for sure what else might be going on. If you approach a situation with an accusatory tone, assuming that the person is lying, they will probably get defensive. They will leave physically or check out mentally from the conversation and you will not learn anything. When you use the Columbo Method, it is more likely that the person will open up and answer your questions honestly. The mystery will be solved and the relationship will be intact. (See the "Law of Reflection" in real-world solution 14.)

Prevent Small Problems
from Becoming Big Ones

HAVE YOU EVER been blindsided by a big problem that seemed to come out of nowhere? Well, it may seem that the big problem materialized out of thin air, but the truth is that the big problem was once a small problem that was ignored or neglected. Implementing the following four keys can prevent many big problems.

1. **Uncover the gold.**
   Find out what people want and value most. Many big issues stem from the failure to discover or clarify what people specifically want from the start. In fact, people often focus on what they *think* other people want rather than truly finding out what others *really* want. How often have you watched as someone worked on a project for another person without knowing that person's expectations? Time, resources, and

money are wasted as a result. Even in personal relationships, it is important to find out what the other person wants and values most rather than making assumptions. You know what happens when we assume... By clarifying the definition of success and ensuring that it is consistent with everyone else's definition at the start, we can help prevent many big problems.

2. **Manage expectations.**

   Once we've learned what someone *really* wants, we need to be upfront and realistic about whether it can be delivered. If the person's expectations are vague or unreasonable, let them know immediately. Although this may be upsetting, it is not nearly as upsetting as it would be if you failed to meet their expectations. Negotiate and agree on achieveable expectations. Often, people and organizations do not receive rewards for their hard work, because they did not manage expectations upfront — *before* they began working on a project. The key is to set it up so you can win — but to win the race we need to know where the finish line is. Establish a reputation for being upfront about expectations, and you will build a trusting relationship that will pay dividends in the future. Remember the golden rule of customer service and dealing with others: under-promise and over-deliver!

3. **Get ahead of the curve.**

   Proactively bring up difficult issues and information before they are discovered. Bad news about you or your organization is received better if it comes directly from your mouth than from someone else's. If someone else discovers bad news before you divulge it, your trustworthiness and credibility are undermined. This may also result in the other party micromanaging the situation because the trust has disappeared. When there is bad news, say so. People may be upset about the news, but they will be more likely to trust you if you are proactive about sharing it and have a plan for fixing the problem. As someone once said, "It can take years to build trust and loyalty, but it only takes a minute to lose it." Get ahead of the curve on bad news.

4. **Go fishing.**
   Check in and ask questions to see how things are going. If you sense that the other person has an issue with something, even if they are not verbalizing it, "go fishing" by asking probing questions. There are many ways to discover hidden issues. You can ask, "On a scale of 1 to 10, how would you rate our relationship on the project?" Then ask, "What would it take to make it a 10?" (If they answered, "10," then ask, "What would it take to make it a 15?") One reason people don't usually ask questions like these is because they are afraid of the answers. I find this ironic. Problems cannot be addressed, let alone resolved, unless you know about them. So remember, if in doubt, check it out.

When you uncover the gold, manage expectations, get ahead of the curve, and go fishing, you can prevent big problems for yourself and for others. These keys will allow you to save time, improve performance, and accomplish your goals. Follow these steps so small problems don't become big ones.

Prevent Sidetracked Conversations

HAS ANYONE EVER said something they know is irritating to you to divert the conversation away from the real issue? It has happened to all of us. Afterward, you walk away and think, "I don't think they ever addressed my original issue."

For instance, have you confronted someone about turning something in late, and instead of addressing the issue, they respond by reminding you of the things you did not complete on time? They do this to push your buttons, distract from the real issue, and send the conversation down an entirely different path.

Welcome to the world of red herrings. A red herring is something that diverts attention from the issue at hand. In communication, a red herring is a phrase or comment that sounds meaningful and important, but it really just throws the listener off track and leads the conversation down a diverted path.

If you've ever confronted someone about their behavior and they responded, "That's just the way I am," then you've encountered a red herring. Consider their response. What does it *really* mean? Does it mean that the person is predisposed or genetically wired to always do something a certain way? The truth is that people can change if they truly want to, and often they just don't want to — but it doesn't sound good to admit that. So, they respond with what sounds like a real excuse. But of course, it is really just a red herring.

Here are three ways to handle the red herring:

1. **Ignore it and focus on the issue at hand.**
    If someone says, "It's just the way I am. I am always late." You reply, "Okay. Are you going to get the report to me on time by three this afternoon?" Don't allow yourself to get pulled down a dead-end road by a red herring. Notice that there was no response to the comment, "It's just the way I am. I am always late." There is no need to comment. The issue is the report. Re-focus the conversation to resolve the issue at hand. Repeat yourself if necessary. This technique is especially useful when people say things that they think will get your goat. Just ignore it and focus on the objective of the conversation.

2. **Question it using the Columbo Method.**
    You could say something like, "I'm confused. You said you would get the report to me by 3:00 P.M. Are you going to give it to me on time?" By acknowledging that you are confused, you are acknowledging that their red herring comment does not have to do with the issue at hand. This also allows you to restate the original question.

3. **Use the million-dollar test.**

   Ask the person, "If I were able to give you a million dollars to give me the report on time, would you give it to me on time?" The person would likely say, "Well, yes, but you don't have a million dollars." Your response would be, "Exactly. You could give me the report on time if you really wanted to. So what's it going to take so that I can count on this report coming in on time?" In other words, it is a question of desire and commitment — not a question of ability. The truth is that most people can change just about anything if they are really willing to. The question is: Are they willing?

No one can throw you off track unless you allow him or her to do so. It is up to you to take control of the issues and refocus conversations. You can make it happen and get the results you want by not falling for the red herrings.

Eliminate Distortion, Rumors, and Hearsay

WHY IS LISTENING so difficult, and what can we do about it? Why do rumors and hearsay continue, and how do we stop them? The first step is to uncover the root of these problems, which in turn will provide some solutions.

PROBLEM ONE: PEOPLE DON'T LISTEN

Although studies differ on the matter, many conclude that people speak about 150 to 200 words per minute and think at least 600 words per minute — and probably a lot faster than that. Whatever the research, it is universally accepted that we all think faster than we speak. Therein lies the challenge. Our brains operate significantly faster than the rate at which someone can speak.

When we're listening to someone, we have the time to add a significant amount to what that person is actually saying to us. We think. We add those extra words. We interpret. We twist. We alter the message! After all, a brain has got to do something with all that extra time!

While your boss or your spouse or your best friend is talking, your brain is chugging along, embroidering all manner of frills and lace around the edges of the real message. While your brain is doing all this tinkering with the incoming words, it is also repeatedly hitting the save button, dumping the whole thing — the real words *and* the embroidery — into your memory. The problem is that your brain doesn't bother to separate that information.

So there is just this one file labeled: "Conversation Last Monday with Sally about the New Project," and everything gets dumped into the file willy-nilly. On Friday afternoon, when you sit down to sort out that conversation about that critical new project, you mentally open the file and start removing pieces of information — without the slightest clue whether the information you're extracting is what Sally actually said or some bit of word juggling your bored, overactive mind produced. This is a primary way that misunderstandings come about. Sally said X and you think she said Y — and you remember it quite clearly!

To make matters worse, I recently read one study that said the average attention span of a human being is eight seconds. So, when something you hear triggers a thought, your excess mental capacity wanders off to follow that trail to another thought, then another thought, then another thought... and suddenly you're daydreaming instead of paying attention to what is really being said.

So we alter the messages we hear *and* our tiny attention spans won't even let us completely hear anything without disconnecting and wandering. It is a miracle that any messages get through at all. So it's true — people don't listen. If individuals and organizations would simply operate with that understanding, we would all be a lot better off.

PROBLEM TWO: HEARSAY IS ALWAYS DISTORTED

Unfortunately, we tend to forget all about childhood games as we get older. But we would all do well to remember the game of telephone and what a kick we got out of the distorted message at the end of the telephone line.

The truth is that we encounter an adult version of this phenomenon in the workplace, but we seem to have forgotten the point of the game — that messages passed from one person to the next get distorted. In fact, in our workplaces, we often think hearsay information is... the truth!

Let's be conservative, and for the sake of this point, assume that people speak at 200 words per minute and people think at 600 words per minute. (The discrepancy is probably a lot worse.) Even in this scenario, we can say that when we tell one person what another person said — hearsay only one person removed — the message is garbled, possibly up to and maybe even exceeding, a factor of four. The reason is this: in the 200/600 dichotomy, we have time to add four hundred words to what someone is saying to us – two times the original amount. If we pass what we "heard" along to someone else, they in turn may add their own additional 400 words to what just said, thus creating a factor of four. And that doesn't even account for exacerbating factors — such as a listener's animosity or preoccupation. Such factors could further distort the communicated information.

Let's face it: when someone tells you what someone else said, it is *always* distorted — and that is just one person removed! But real life dictates that things usually don't stop there. In real life that one person tells someone else who in turn tells someone else. That is why the role of "ambassador" in the workplace is problematic.

Allow me to examine a typical scenario in which this dynamic plays out. A project manager often acts as an ambassador between the client and the project staff. So the project manager meets with the customer to find out the customer's desires, goals, and expectations. Later the project manager holds a meeting to inform the project staff what the customer wants. What happens? You guessed it, the information is distorted. In fact, the real-world scenario may be worse. A project manager doesn't usually get a chance to meet directly with the client. Instead the project manager meets with the client's assistant. Thus, the client tells the assistant to tell the project manager who tells the people who work on the project what the client wants. It is a miracle that anything is accomplished accurately at all! The truth is — a lot of the time it doesn't. And the cost is enormous in terms of productivity, profitability, stress, and decreased morale.

SOLUTIONS

Lack of listening and hearsay information are real problems and should not be ignored. Rather than wishing the problems didn't exist, follow these twelve rules, and you will see a huge difference.

1. Check out rumors by going directly to the source.

2. Don't pass rumors on.

3. To ensure clarity, paraphrase back to people what you hear them say and have people paraphrase your statements back to you.

4. Take notes and document what someone says in a conversation. Have them verify the documentation is correct. Remember, in a dispute, whoever has the most documentation usually wins!

5. Repeat and summarize your message.

6. Keep messages as short and simple as possible. Let the details follow your main message, just as newspaper articles are written.

7. Establish frequent milestone meetings to make sure everyone is on the same page. If the project is moving along successfully, you can decrease the frequency of the meetings.

8. Develop a powerful network within your organization so you can crosscheck the information you receive.

9. If you manage people, pass on information in a lot of different ways (verbal reports, written reports, memos, e-mails, town-hall meetings, websites, etc.) to ensure that people at all levels receive the true message.

10. If you manage people, check in with people at all levels to ensure the information they are receiving is accurate and to hear feedback.

11. If possible, do not act as an ambassador. Instead, coach, support, and encourage people to talk directly with each other — especially when they have a problem with each other. If need be, facilitate a meeting between the two parties.

12. Eliminate distractions. When someone is talking to you, do not file, type, or perform any other activities. If you are on a conference call, exit out of your e-mail program or, better yet, turn your monitor off. Remember, it is hard enough to concentrate on what someone is saying without distractions. If you work with someone who gets easily distracted,

try to have any meetings with that person in an area with few distractions.

If we accept and remember that people don't listen and that hearsay information is always distorted, we can develop procedures, processes, and systems that in the end will make everyone's life easier and more productive. These twelve rules will set you on your way. Don't just *think* about implementing them, *do it*. You can make the difference!

The 5-Step Relationship Checkup

IS SOMEONE IN your life not listening to you? Does this cause friction and difficulty? Are the two of you struggling to get along? I had a seminar participant who complained that his teenage daughter wasn't listening to him. I asked him a simple question: "If your daughter was in the next room and I asked her if she thought her dad listened to her, what would she say?" He grinned and candidly admitted that she probably would say he didn't listen to her either. I then asked him: "How likely is it that your daughter will listen to you if she feels that you don't listen to her?" After careful consideration, he agreed it was unlikely. People want to be heard, and since you can only control your own actions, you must listen first.

If someone isn't listening to you, you can begin to significantly improve the situation by using the Five-Step Relationship Checkup Process™. Just as you go to a doctor for periodic checkups, you should perform a checkup on your relationships to reveal hidden problems and find appropriate solutions to those problems. This process is especially helpful if you feel someone isn't listening to you, or you're not getting helpful feedback, or the person is unwilling to open their mind to hear what *you* are saying.

THE FIVE-STEP RELATIONSHIP CHECKUP PROCESS™

1. **Be direct and ask, "Do you think I listen to you — *really* listen to you?"**
   The point is to ask a very direct, clear question.

2. **Admit the truth if you don't listen.**
   If you take an honest look at yourself, you would probably admit that you are not always *really* listening to the other person. Once you realize this, you might be afraid to admit it. Don't worry. They already know. Can't *you* tell when someone isn't listening to you? By proactively admitting the truth, the person will notice that your conversations are more honest and upfront than they have been in the past. Also, being truthful will encourage the other person to be truthful with you.

3. **Ask, "What can I do (or we do) to improve things from this point forward?"**
   This question puts the focus on exploring solutions rather than finding out who is to blame. A participant in one of my seminars took her ten-year-old daughter through this process. When the mother asked what could she do to improve things, her daughter replied, "It would be great if you could look me in the eyes, rather than cooking dinner, when you are asking me how school is going." Remember,

when you ask for feedback, some people may have a hard time admitting things to you. It's particularly difficult if you already have challenges with them, so do your best to create a safe environment for them. Do not debate them when they start to give you feedback. Instead, just be a sponge and try to soak it all in. This will allow the person to fully express what they are thinking. In my experience, initial feedback comments are really just tests to gauge your potential reaction. The real feedback will follow once they feel safe that you won't react negatively.

4. **Make commitments.**

   Unilaterally commit to some action on your part to improve the relationship. This will often inspire the other person to take action too. Even if they don't, you can still move things forward by making a commitment and being proactive. For example, you might tell the other person that, from now on, you will admit when it is a bad time to talk instead of pretending to listen. Or tell them you won't try to watch TV or read the paper while you are listening. If it's a person at work, you might tell them that you won't read e-mail or conduct other business while they are talking.

5. **Follow up.**

   Plan a time to check in to verify that the committed action items were accomplished to everyone's satisfaction. This will give the relationship some positive forward momentum and likely inspire further action. Following up may require you to go back to step one and repeat the entire process. No matter what, don't wait to follow up. It is better to do this sooner rather than later — even if it doesn't feel like the most opportune time.

Difficult relationships are usually the result of repeated communication problems that are ignored or are not immediately resolved. The difficulty didn't develop overnight and the repair won't either. However, repeated efforts at using this process can turn night into day.

So, relationships that have had a lot of issues may need to run through the Five-Step Relationship Checkup Process™ several times. Until the people in our lives truly believe we hear them, it's unlikely they'll be willing to hear us. Better to do the checkup now than to have major problems down the road. By using these strategies, you can take steps toward developing the healthy, productive, and fulfilling relationships that you deserve.

Instantly Enhance
Any Relationship

THE LAW OF REFLECTION is the key to instantly changing and enhancing
any relationship. This law states that what we give out is what we
tend to get back. We have all different versions of this: the golden
rule, do unto others as you would have them do unto you, what
goes around, comes around, and we reap what we sow. In fact, it is
amazing how prevalent this basic lesson is in various religions and
philosophies.

Let's see if this law really holds true. When people are upset
with us, we tend to get upset with them; when people blame us,
we tend to blame them; when people accuse us, we tend to
accuse them right back. It also tends to hold true in the positive
direction. When people take responsibility for their actions, we
tend to take responsibility for ours; when people apologize, we
tend to apologize back.

Of course, this isn't always true. For instance, sometimes we apologize to someone and the person says, "Well, I am glad you finally admitted it." However, even in those situations, aggression toward us usually diminishes.

We can even see the Law of Reflection in a group's response to a leader. A sports team's style and ability to win often changes when a new coach is brought in. A business group's productivity often soars or plummets when a new executive or manager is hired.

When I work with groups, I can usually predict the attitude of the leader by interviewing the people who report directly to that leader. When the group blames, I usually find that the boss is a blamer as well. When the employees have an attitude of taking full responsibility, I usually find that the boss possesses this same attitude. The Law of Reflection is often the reason an organization makes a change in leadership.

This law also holds true within groups. If a new hire is placed on your team and that individual is particularly negative, the entire morale and productivity of the team may diminish. Or when someone particularly enthusiastic is hired as part of the team, the team may become more energetic and motivated.

That's pretty exciting, because it reminds us of the power of the individual. One person *can* and *will* make a difference if they focus on what they can do to help the team. The problem is that often people think, *What difference can I make? I am only one person.* At that moment, they are forgetting about the Law of Reflection and the positive impact they can have by concentrating on their individual actions.

Two of my favorite examples of the power of the Law of Reflection are Reverend Martin Luther King, Jr., and Mahatma Gandhi. Although neither held political office, they quite literally changed the world by what they said and how they behaved.

When faced with insurmountable odds, they chose to focus on what they *could* do and took action accordingly. If people can change the world using this principle, we can change our own world if we really want to.

Unfortunately, when we have a problem with someone, we tend to focus on that person — whom we have no control over — rather than focusing on ourselves — the only person we can control. Even if you didn't start the problem, you can be the one to fix it. What counts most is what you are willing to do about the situation. One of my seminar participants shared a breakthrough he had in his marriage. He said that his first two years of marriage were awful for one primary reason: he had gone into the marriage believing that it was a 50/50 proposition — he gives 50 percent, she gives 50 percent, and together they would compromise. After some professional counseling, he discovered that the key to marriage (as well as most relationships) is to give 100 percent on his own — regardless of what his spouse was giving. So he began to give 100 percent and the Law of Reflection took hold. His wife started to give 100 percent as well.

Consider this — even if only one person gives 100 percent and the other doesn't change at all, the situation has still improved. If things don't turn out as planned, at least we can say, "I gave it my all. At least I gave it 100 percent," instead of being plagued with doubts.

Applying the Law of Reflection is also the key to compelling people to be more honest with us. A seminar participant once complained to me that her elderly father, with whom she has tried to develop a close relationship, wouldn't ever truly open up to her no matter how much she shared with him. I asked her to consider that she may be sharing a lot, while not really being honest. Suddenly, her face changed to sadness and she said, "I know what it is. I am not sharing with him that I wonder if he approves of the way I am living my life and that his approval is important to me. Instead I have only shared my accomplishments, hoping that he would voice his approval." She left the seminar that day with a plan to tell her father the truth and begin a new relationship with him.

If we want to change the dynamics of a relationship, it is important for us to take the first step. Concentrating on the one person we can control — ourselves — and responding honestly often starts us down a new path to the relationships we desire.

The Greatest Gift You Can Give

IT IS NOT only important to share difficult messages but to be open and honest with others about what you appreciate. It is one of the greatest gifts that you can give someone. My grandfather lived in a nursing home during the last several years of his life before passing away three months shy of his one hundredth birthday. During one of my visits to see him, a nurse pulled me aside and told me what a great man my grandfather was. I appreciated that and asked her why she thought so. She responded, "He is the only person here who always says thank you."

And that's the power of thank you. *Thank you* may be just two words in the English language, but those words mean so much to so many people. To this nurse, they meant everything.

My grandfather always acknowledged people. He acknowledged small things. During my last visit with him the night before he passed away, I saw him thank the nurse for helping him with his hearing aid. He acknowledged large things too. He referred to his daughter, my mother, as an angel for visiting him daily and making him feel loved and inspired to face the challenge of another day.

Why is being honest about your acknowledgement and appreciation so important? It serves two purposes. First, it shows people that they *can* make a difference. I believe that the driving force for most human beings is the desire to make a difference. We want to know that our lives count, and we need to feel like we matter to someone. As Benjamin Disraeli said, "The greatest good you can do for another is not to share your riches, but to reveal theirs."

Many of us work extra hours, often for no additional money or benefit. Why? Because we want to make a difference in our jobs, and we want to contribute. In fact, through conducting career development seminars, I have learned that one of the biggest fears that people seem to have in common is the fear of dying without making a difference. Many parents have shared with me how consumed they are with making sure they are really making a difference in their children's lives. So when you acknowledge someone, you are basically saying, "I notice you. You are important. You are significant. You are making a difference."

The second purpose of acknowledgement is that it makes someone feel better about themselves. When we acknowledge someone, we have to think positively, at least for that moment. The more we acknowledge and appreciate others, the more positive moments we have. Over time, that makes us feel better about those around us and about ourselves. If you consistently feel sad, make a concerted effort to acknowledge the people around you. You will start to feel better and your attitude will improve.

Yes, sometimes acknowledgements feel awkward. That's because we might not be used to expressing them. For many of us, saying thank you means letting down our guard, showing that we care, or letting someone know what we think and feel. Some people become stingy with their compliments. They fear that if they compliment too much, their compliments will be less valuable. This isn't something most of us need to worry about. In fact, I have never heard of someone leaving an organization because he or she was acknowledged *too* much. But we have all heard of people leaving organizations because they were not appreciated *enough*.

FOUR KEYS TO ACKNOWLEDGEMENT

To ensure that your acknowledgement and praise have a significant impact, implement the following four keys. Remember the ISOS acronym.

- I = Immediate
  Even if it is over the phone or via e-mail, express your appreciation immediately. Often we want to do something special to show our appreciation, but that can take time. It's important to do something quickly, even if it is something small. You can always do something special later. If you don't do anything immediately, the person you really do appreciate may feel unappreciated. Seize the moment and do it right away.

- S = Specific
  Make the acknowledgement specific. Rather than saying, "Thanks for all your help," say, "Thanks for the detail you put into the report. It obviously took a tremendous amount of time and dedication." Being specific adds importance and validity to the acknowledgement.

- O = Often
  As we discussed previously, few have ever suffered from too much acknowledgement, but many have suffered because

there was not enough. Don't be stingy. Offer it frequently, appropriately, and creatively.

- S = Sincere
  Say it only if you mean it. People are smart, and they can tell if you are faking it. A sincere acknowledgement that comes from the heart is a powerful motivator.

MAKE IT A HABIT

To successfully develop the habit of acknowledging others, commit to acknowledging five people a day for one month. Each day, place five pennies in your left-hand pocket. Every time you acknowledge or compliment someone, move one penny from your left pocket to your right. The goal is to move all five pennies by the end of the day. At the end of the day, put a dollar in a jar for every penny that you did not move.

For the second month, put ten pennies in your pocket each morning and continue to put a dollar in the jar for every penny not moved by the end of the day. At the end of the two months, take the money in the jar and buy something for the most important person in your life and give it to them.

The gift of acknowledgement is the greatest gift you can give someone. Tell someone today what a difference they have made in your life. Then watch the difference you make in theirs.

Discover What Others Really *Want*

AN IMPORTANT KEY to making and keeping customers (including your boss, co-workers, employees, spouse, children, relatives, and so on) happy is to discover what they really want and value most. This will help you manage their expectations and decide whether or not you can provide this for them.

When you are working on a project, confirm the criteria for success. Determine what is most important to the client, the boss, and the rest of the team. Be sure your definition of success is consistent with everyone else's definition of success! People often tend to work on what *they* think is important and what they *perceive* others think is important, not necessarily what others really *do* think is important.

WHAT TO DO IF SOMEONE IS VAGUE OR SOUNDS UNSURE

Sometimes when we ask someone what they want, they say they aren't sure or act confused about what want. But the truth is that many people are not as confused or unsure as they imply. So, why do they say they are? By remaining confused or unsure, these people won't have to be accountable for what they say they want. If they are clear about what they want and we deliver it to them, then they will feel accountable about being satisfied. People may not necessarily be conscious of this; they may have just not thought it through.

With a few techniques, we can break through the confusion, uncertainty, and the *I don't knows*. Think of the human mind as a computer that contains the correct security code to access the data. The following six techniques (in varying combinations) will help you get the security code that will unlock the data (what that person really wants). One word of caution — these techniques will only work if someone *allows* what they really want to be uncovered. Make sure you gauge their desire before proceeding.

1. **Put an *IF* in front of the objection, make it a positive, and ask them for their hunch.**

   If they say, "I am unsure," you respond, "If you *were* sure, what would your hunch be?" If a person says, "I don't know what I want," you say, "If you did know what you wanted, what would your hunch be?" If they say, "I am confused," you say, "If you weren't confused, what would your hunch be?" One reason this technique works is that it helps the person remove or work around what they are mentally fixated on. When we become fixated on the objections (the confusion), we lose sight of the ultimate goal. By reframing the question, and thereby removing the objection with a "what if" question, we actually show the other person a path around the objection, allowing that person to see what he or she really wants. This technique allows the person to think about what they would do if the objection wasn't there. Don't be afraid of a little silence here. Let the other person think through their answer! Once a person has a little time to think and reflect with the objection removed, then that person may eventually say, "Well, I guess I would..." Extremely important: If the person verbalizes what they want and you want to gauge how certain they are about that decision, ask them, "Under what circumstances would you change your mind?" For example, one participant shared his uncertainty about whether he and his wife should have another child. I asked, "If you were certain of your decision, what might be your hunch?" He answered, "Yes." Then I asked, "What would change your mind?" He gave a litany of issues such as, "If my wife was not really excited about having another child," "If our finances were low," and so on. Once each of the issues was clear, I said, "If these things were resolved would you then have a child?" He said, "Yes." He now knew the specific issues he needed to address with his wife in order to move forward. Also the question, "What would change your mind?" is a wonderful question to ask someone who is a decision maker to gauge and account for possible issues, problems, and challenges that may eventually arise. This will help you in the development and execution of your plans.

2. **Ask, "What don't you want?"**
   People often have trouble saying what they want, but they usually have no trouble saying what they *don't* want. For example, if someone is unsure about what they want to do about their career, ask them what they don't want to happen

in their career. Interestingly enough, if you wait long enough for them to exhaust their list, eventually they begin to share ideas of what they *do* want. Similar to the first technique, a little silence on our part can go a long way. This allows time for them to reveal what they really want. Even if they only list things they say they don't want, you can still take their comments and reverse them into what they *do* want. For example, "I don't want you to take forty-eight hours to return my call." Their expectation is for you to return their call in less than forty-eight hours. You can also use their response to ask a more direct, goal-oriented question, such as, "In what time frame would you prefer for me to return your call?"

3. **Use the magic wand.**
Say, "If I gave you a magic wand, what would you want?" People are often afraid to ask us for what they really want, because they are afraid of our response. A magic wand gives them the freedom to be creative. This way, you can find out what they really want and then work your way through what can be delivered. You can also use the magic wand technique on yourself to bring clarity to a situation. For example, when a client asks for help and I am unsure of all of the possible limiting factors and constraints, I will say, "If I had a magic wand, I would suggest we do…" This becomes a starting point for the discussion about how my company can be of assistance and really help them take care of their problems.

4. **Go forward in time.**
Ask, "If you were ninety years old and looking back at this situation, what would you want to say had happened?" This

technique works well with some people who are stuck in the past or the present. Jumping them to the distant future allows them to get out of the day's worries and concerns and think of the big picture.

5. **Ask them, "Can you paint a picture for me of how that would look?"**
   This technique is often used in conjunction with the first three, when the person is vague about what they want. They may say things such as, "to do a good job," "to work hard," "to be sensitive to what the customer wants," or "to have a better relationship." These phrases lack specifics and are subjective. It is critical to clarify exactly what they mean by probing with questions about how it would look or how you would measure it. By doing so, the person starts to construct mental pictures of what they want, which in turn helps them explain it to you.

6. **Make suggestions and give options.**
   If someone still has trouble being specific, make some suggestions to help them gain clarity and understanding. Sometimes people are not the best at creating something from nothing, but if you prod them a little and give them some things to think about, you can help them figure out what they really want. Of course, it is impossible to make other people tell us what they want if they don't wish to. But by using these techniques, you can help someone access and uncover what they truly want. This, in turn, helps us manage expectations and accomplish what needs to be accomplished.

7 *Ingredients for Career Success*

WHEN IT COMES to our career success, we are often not honest with ourselves about reality and what needs to be done to take our career to the next level. After all, *we* are responsible for our own careers — not our boss, not our co-workers, not the human resources department, and not our significant other. If we are responsible, then we are the ones who are going to have to do something about it. Examine the following seven essential ingredients to career success and honestly rate yourself on a scale of 1 to 10 (1 being the worst and 10 being the best) to see what area you really need to focus on.

1. **Know where you want to go.**
   If you are not sure where you are going, you may drift in a direction that wastes your time and does not bring you the joy and fulfillment you desire.

2. **Know where you are.**

   You must know where you *are* in order to plan how to get where you want to be. In your assessment, be honest about what you currently think about yourself, the people around you, and your situation.

3. **Let the past go.**

   Stop dragging your failures around every day. Learn from the lessons of the past that will be helpful and move on. Don't get stuck in the memories of how you were wronged. Give it up and move on. Life has never been fair and will never be fair. Let go of the past and enjoy your life.

4. **Focus on what you can control.**

   Since you can't control other people, concentrate on what you *can* control — yourself and your responses. When confronted with a problem, one of the most important questions you can ask yourself is: "What am I willing and going to do about it?" Answering this question will help you focus on what you can do to resolve issues and reach your goals.

5. **Be coachable.**

   Be willing to listen and learn from everyone. For example, when you receive negative feedback, be careful not to shoot the messenger. Resist the temptation to dismiss advice from someone you may not like. Instead, try on the feedback like you would try on a hat and see if it fits. Consider whether there is anything you can take away from the feedback that will be helpful. Often the feedback we get defensive about is the feedback we really need to be listening to.

6. **Be committed.**

Commitment is about taking action based on what you said you would do, despite how you feel about it at the moment. Be committed to doing whatever you must do to accomplish your goal. What if failing is not an option? If you really want to be committed, tell people you are going to do something and ask them to hold you accountable for doing it.

7. **Take action.**

Planning is good, but action is the key. This is where the doers separate themselves from the talkers. We've all spent time talking about an idea but not acting on it, only to find out later that someone had a similar idea, implemented it, and reaped the rewards. Taking action is essential to accomplishing our goals. Remember, some action is better than no action. If need be, you can change, reverse, or alter your course later. The key is to take at least some action *now*.

Now that you have rated yourself, pick the lowest score. Share those scores with five people and ask them for their advice. Then choose three specific actions that you will do based on this advice. Ask someone to hold you accountable and then do the things you need to do. For extra motivation (and for accountability reasons) set up a consequence for not following through.

The only person you can control is you. Take full responsibility for your career success. Make things happen and enjoy the ride to the next level of your career. It will take commitment and hard work, but if you are ready, you can climb the ladder of success — however you define it! (See the "Seven Steps to Forgiveness Freedom™" in real-world solution 25 and "How to Receive Difficult Feedback" in real-world solution 33.)

Create the Relationship You Want

DURING THE COURSE of each day without even realizing it, we train and condition people how to respond to us. Unfortunately, we often encourage individuals to act in ways that we did not intend, failing to recognize the messages that we send through our own actions.

How are you conditioning people? Do you say it is important to be on time and then start your meeting late? Are you asking people to be upfront but get defensive when they are? If so, you are encouraging people to do the opposite of what you say you really want.

Let's examine two common problems — missed deadlines and lack of honesty — and see how reconditioning might work.

MISSED DEADLINES

If you tell someone a report is due at 3:00 P.M. and it arrives at 5:00 P.M., would you say something about it? If you don't, then you're conditioning them that your deadlines are *flexible* and what you say is not what you mean. Over time, people will lose faith in your words and the situation will worsen.

How are you training people to deal with your deadlines? If someone is upfront that they cannot make the original deadline, how do you react? If you respond in a defensive or negative manner, your reaction encourages them (and possibly trains them) to be less upfront with you in the future.

We need to create an open environment for people to respond truthfully about whether they will achieve their deadlines. Then we need to respond in an appropriate way if they don't do what they say they were going to do. Again, suppose the deadline is 3:00 P.M. You could call them at 1:00 P.M. to see how things are going, or as 3:00 P.M. passes, you could call them to find out where the report is. If indeed they miss the deadline, you could let them know you will have to start to document these misses. Again, this may sound harsh, but we owe it to ourselves and others who might be affected to hold everyone accountable to the same expectations.

LACK OF HONESTY

As strange as it may sound, we can teach people to be honest with us or we can teach them to be dishonest with us. This happens in all kind of ways, and we've already discussed a few of them. Let's look at another scenario. When someone is not honest with us, we need to ask ourselves what it is about us that makes the other person want to hide the truth?

A manager who had been demoted took my class, and he was bitter. His whole staff, he said, never said a word to him about any problems. Instead, his staff complained to his boss, who in turn demoted him. I suggested he go back and interview his former staff to try to find out what he had done that caused them not to come to him with problems and concerns.

To his credit, he did exactly that. And what he uncovered explained it all. He learned that his staff thought he did not care about them, because he never left his office to go see them. He also learned that when they came to see him, he was always too busy and never seemed to have the time to talk.

Ironically, the reason he remained in his office and did not check in with his staff was that he didn't want them to think he was micromanaging them. Of course, he didn't bother to tell them that! And the reason he was so busy was that he was lining up new contracts to guarantee that his staff wouldn't be downsized. Of course, he didn't tell them that either! After receiving this feedback, he went to his boss and took responsibility for his actions. He asked what he had to do to get his job back.

Years ago, I was at our traditional Thanksgiving Day family get-together, and I overheard my mother say to one of my relatives that my father had shingles (an adult version of the chicken pox). It stopped me cold. Although I frequently call my parents, this was the first I had heard of my dad having shingles. I confronted my mom and asked, "What was it about me that made you feel like you could not tell me the truth?"

Her response stunned and enlightened me. She said that I always prefaced my calls with how I was just leaving this place or going to that place or getting on this airplane or off that airplane, and she just didn't think I had the time or that I was really willing to listen. She said my calls sounded as if I were just checking something off a checklist.

You know what? That's exactly what I was doing. My mom was absolutely right. Now before I ask a question, I ask myself, do I really want to hear the answer? We often say we want to listen.

We often say we want people to be honest but then send an entirely different message.

As you can see, there are a lot of ways we can condition others to be dishonest with us. What lessons in honesty are you teaching the people in your life? The only person you can control is yourself. The key is to take action that sends the message you want and produces the outcome you desire.

THE TRAIN AND CONDITION RESULTS METHOD™

It may be upsetting to realize you have conditioned people to do things you don't want them to, but the good news is that you can do something about it. If you have been silent, you need to be more vocal. If you have been inconsistent, you need to be more predictable. If you have been getting defensive, you might need to apologize and really listen to and hear the feedback you are receiving.

The following five-step process, the Train and Condition Results Method™, can help shift old patterns of communication from unhealthy ones to healthy ones.

1. **Take sincere responsibility for your contribution to the situation.**

   For example, if your staff is having a problem with deadlines, maybe you were unclear when you gave the time frame. Maybe you used vague words and phrases such as "try to" or "ASAP" or "it's no big deal, but if you wouldn't mind…" Maybe you were silent when a deadline came and went, giving the person the impression that the deadline was flexible rather than urgent. The key is not to blame others. This lack of blame will reduce their defensiveness, so they can really hear what you are saying. By taking responsibility, you will encourage others to take a look at themselves without forcing them to. This will pave the way to finding a workable solution.

2. **Ask what can be done from this point forward to resolve the situation.**
   People who take part in creating a solution are more likely to implement it. If other people have a hard time coming up with ideas, you might jump start things by offering suggestions. With regard to tardiness at meetings, you might suggest starting a meeting at a different time when everyone can promise to be there. For missed deadlines, you might suggest milestone meetings to check in and ensure everything is on track. More than likely, everyone will have good ideas to contribute if we just ask.

3. **Decide on an agreeable, specific plan of action to resolve the issue.**
   This provides further clarification and allows for a final opportunity to iron out potential problems. In addition, this sends the message that you are serious about changing the situation.

4. **Clearly define the benefits of change and the costs or consequences if things do not change.**
   The universal language we all speak is, "What's in it for me?" The key is to let others know what the benefits are for them to change. With missed deadlines, you might want to be clear and upfront with a consequence if the problem continues (such as documentation that would go in their employee file). Knowledge of the person and the situation should help you determine the appropriate benefit or consequence.

5. **If the behavior happens again, follow the plan and take action.**

   Make sure you follow through with the consequences you've outlined. Otherwise, you will reinforce the conditioning that you don't mean what you say. The key is to be persistent, follow through, and hold people accountable. This will make it clear that you are committed to change.

Understanding that we condition people how to deal with us and taking responsibility for this is crucial to getting the results we want. If we've trained them incorrectly, we can always re-train them. Remember, the key question is what are we going to do about it? By applying the Train and Condition Results Method™, you can send the appropriate message, produce the change, and make the difference. (See the "Law of Reflection" in real-world solution 14 and "MT. SAMIE" in real-world solution 4.)

5 Keys to Effectively Sharing Your Viewpoint

DEEP DOWN INSIDE, most people think they're always right. People often act as if they are open to the idea that they may be wrong about something, even when they don't think that's even remotely possible. The problem is this: if each person in a disagreement believes they are right, it can be very difficult to resolve issues with one another. The result can be constant bickering, frustration, and a lot of anger with little resolution.

Here are five keys to effectively sharing your point of view for the purpose of resolving issues.

1. **Be open to the possibility that you are wrong — really be open to it.**
   Understand and operate as if your assumptions, opinions, and conclusions are exactly that — assumptions, opinions, and conclusions that may be incorrect. Believing we may be

wrong may be hard to admit, but think about how often people are wrong about us. If others are wrong about us, we can only logically deduce that we are probably wrong about our assumptions, opinions, and conclusions about others more often than we realize. If this idea still seems hard to accept, remember that we tend to look for evidence to support our opinions. We see what we want to see, believe what we want to believe, and remember what we want to remember. We also rationalize or forget all the times we have been wrong. For example, once we label someone as difficult, that is all we tend to notice. If that *difficult* person compliments us, we think they are up to something, even though they may just be trying to better the relationship. If we really are open to the possibility that we are wrong, we are more likely to open our eyes and notice things we would otherwise miss. The first key opens us up to the second key, which is instrumental in all great relationships.

2. **Check in.**

In other words, verify whether your assumptions, opinions, and conclusions are correct by asking questions. This may seem obvious, but it is often overlooked. Has anyone ever acted on their opinion of you as if it were fact, without first checking in with you? You probably said to yourself, "If they had just asked me, I could have corrected the problem." If we check in with each other, this opens up the lines of communication and helps prevent false assumptions, opinions, and conclusions. The more we check in with others, the more likely they will check in with us. Here is the irony: The more open we are to the fact that we may be wrong, the better our life will be. The more we understand that we may be wrong, the more likely we will check in and get the facts.

The more we find out the facts, the better our decisions will become. The better our decisions become, the better our life will become. Utilize any of the following five questions to help you check or investigate your assumptions, opinions, and conclusions about someone or some situation.

- In my mind, I am thinking _____. Is that correct?

- What are your thoughts about this situation?

- I have a lot of opinions about what has happened, so what would you suggest we do? (This is a great way to acknowledge that you have a lot of thoughts without having to immediately express them. This way, you can use the time to find a solution.)

- Given everything that has gone on, where should we go from here? What is the next step?

- On a scale of 1 to 10, how would you rate this project/our work relationship/my job performance? What would make it a 10? A 15? (This is a great set of questions that can reveal a lot of hidden information, desires, wants, and opinions and improve the situation.)

It's important to uncover the facts before determining our actions. By finding out what is really going on and basing our decisions on facts rather than assumptions, opinions, or conclusions, we will be more effective and experience less stress.

3. **Offer your assumptions, opinions, and conclusions with the genuine belief you might be wrong.**

   The secret here is that you *must* believe you might be wrong. If you just pretend, this will not work. For example, can you tell when someone is mad at you even though they say they are not? Pretending doesn't work, because most of us are lousy actors and actresses. People are smart and they see right through the charade. This is why individuals who attend communication seminars and learn new words — but do not truly change the way they think — often come across as fake. It all boils down to the fact that they haven't changed what they truly believe. You must sincerely believe that you may be wrong in order to come across like you are really open to another point of view. When you deliver your opinions, assumptions, and conclusions with that attitude, it won't sound like you are being aggressive or blaming someone, because you won't be. This in turn, will encourage the person to be open about hearing your point of view. Who would you rather work with? Someone who thinks they are right all of the time? Or someone who is willing to be wrong? Most of us don't like being around people who act self-righteous — even if they have a good point.

4. **Suggest one thing you could have done differently.**

   If upon retrospection, you discover that you could have helped or improved the situation in some way, you might say, "One thing I could have done differently was to bring up the issue as soon as I realized it was happening." This is a show of good faith. It reveals that you realize you probably have contributed to the problem (not that you are to blame) and now you see things you could have done to change the outcome of the situation. Also, the more you suggest things you could have done differently, the more likely the other person will think of things *they* could have done differently. This will help resolve the situation.

5. **Make a request.**
   Your request should be about how you think this issue could be resolved. Even if the other person doesn't agree, it sends a message that you want to resolve the issue, not just assign blame.

This is how the five keys might sound when you implement them: "I notice the report came in at 5:00 P.M. rather than at 3:00 P.M. I have all kinds of thoughts about this that are probably way off. I am thinking you may have too much on your plate or that I was unclear on what I wanted. I have a lot of opinions about how this issue could be resolved, and one thing I could have done differently was to bring this up when it first happened and not blame you. My request is for us to develop a plan that works for both of us so we can ensure these reports come in on time."

You may not use this exact language, or even all five keys in every situation, but the bottom line is to keep the intention of all five keys. You must clearly communicate that you are open to being wrong and that you want to find a resolution. It is a lot easier to resolve issues when people are not feeling defensive or as if they are being blamed. This allows everyone to focus most of their time and energy on the most important part of the conversation — resolution! (See the "Law of Reflection" in real-world solution 14.)

Be True to Yourself

AFTER MAJOR EVENTS like September 11, 2001, the death of a loved one, or a major illness, we often vow to do things differently. We may promise to talk to someone we have been estranged from or say something important that we have neglected to say.

Perhaps you have made such promises. How is it going? When was the last time you checked in with yourself to make sure you are on track? Are you doing what you said you would do? Are you saying what you said you would say? Or are you still putting it off, rationalizing that someday you will get to it? My grandmother kept delaying a vacation with my grandfather because of her fear of flying. By the time she finally decided to confront her fear and go on vacation, my grandfather had been diagnosed with lung cancer and died shortly thereafter. I am sure many of you are familiar with stories like these.

Here are three actions to get you moving in the right direction.

1. **Choose a goal that is bigger than you are.**

   After September 11, 2001, many of us felt closer to each other. As a nation, we pulled together. Why? Our grief bonded us with a common purpose. Many of our differences seemed miniscule compared to what we needed to do as a country. Having a common bond can be applied to daily life. How? Create a goal that is larger than yourself, larger than your marriage, larger than your family, larger than your team at work. By creating a purpose — a goal larger than you — you are forced to disengage from the small things and engage in the big things — things that are the most important. For example, do you notice how a family in crisis often pulls together? The crisis requires the family to focus on something bigger than their individual or personality differences. Rather than waiting for a crisis to strike, proactively create a goal that is exciting. For example, plan a big family reunion or a celebration that honors all the elder members of your family. Celebrate their wisdom and what they have done for the subsequent generations. You can create big goals at work too. If you're the boss, decide to be the top performing office, area, group, department, or company in your industry. Decide to double sales, double growth, or double productivity. This goal forces the team to put aside small distractions and focus on the larger goals. If you can't think of an inspiring goal, ask for an idea or brainstorm with a group and collectively choose one! Even if you are not in charge at work, you are in charge of your life. Decide to be the very best, most productive, most acclaimed, or most renowned individual in something. A close friend of mine broke his leg in six places. The doctors told him he would be lucky to walk normally again. He decided at that moment to not only recover from the injury but to run a marathon. He not only completed a marathon, he went on to complete an Iron Man triathalon. He is now a nationally known motivational speaker. Someone once said, "Choose a goal not only for what it will bring you, but what it will make of you."

2. **Do what needs to be done.**
   Are you putting off action toward a goal? People often regret not what they did in life but what they didn't do. So, take action. Even a small action can change your life, send it down a different path to bigger things, and open doors you never knew existed.

3. **Say what you need to say.**
   Share what you need to share. Express what you need to express. What goes unexpressed can eat away at us and haunt us. What is expressed can free us and move us forward in ways we never realized.

One of my favorite quotes is by Norman Cousins, who said, "Death is not the greatest loss. The greatest loss is what dies within you while you live." Don't let something die within you while you live. When you reminisce about this moment in time later in life, what do you want to say you did? Remember, we may not be able to choose what happens to us, but we can *always* choose our response to what comes our way.

Overcome Your Fears

FEAR IS A NORMAL and appropriate response to many of the challenges we face in life. The problem comes when fear becomes a reason for not accomplishing something. The reality is that we often do things *in spite* of our fears — we ride scary amusement park rides, meet future in-laws, go on job interviews, or go skydiving. Fear is not the *real* reason we don't do something; it's just an excuse we allow ourselves to use in order to get off the hook and not do something.

For instance, fear of public speaking is one of the top fears people have. Yet many people speak even though they are very afraid. Johnny Carson, Carly Simon, Carol Burnett, and Barbra Streisand all had fears of performing in public — yet, they became very successful. They learned techniques to handle and overcome their fears. The truth is that fear doesn't stop us from doing anything; we stop ourselves.

Here are five tips to help you gain control and overcome your fear.

1. **Channel your fear into useful energy and actions.**
   Don't bottle up that nervous energy; channel it into action, such as preparation or planning. Walter Cronkite said, "It is natural to have butterflies. The secret is to have them fly in formation." For example, if you need to do a presentation, research the group you are going to address; interview key personnel; become clear about what they want; and then practice, practice, practice. Plan and account for potential problems. If you are nervous about a job interview, write down interview questions and answers, then practice them out loud. You might even take a practice ride to the interview location. Don't bottle up your fear — use it.

2. **Share fears out loud, then repeat positive affirmations to yourself.**
   This may feel odd at first, but try it. Vocalize all of your concerns and fears about a situation out loud. Once you get the concerns and fears out, start verbalizing the positive affirmations. For example, say out loud, "It is going to go great," or "They are going to love the presentation." Remember, it is impossible to think positive and negative thoughts at the same time. It is especially hard to think positively when you are thinking negatively. So, share all of your worries and concerns, then share the positive affirmations and watch the magic.

3. **Practice visualization.**
   Visualization is a powerful tool. Do you ever catch yourself daydreaming? Daydreaming is visualization, and you can

apply the same concept to facing fear. Visualize yourself successfully handling the situation you are afraid of. Run that picture through your head at least ten times. Do this in a quiet place with no distractions and your eyes closed. If you can't visualize yourself successfully facing a fearful situation, imagine you are in a movie theatre watching someone who looks like you, acts like you, and talks like you handling the situation successfully. Do this at least ten times. After you complete this visualization, put yourself back into the picture and run through the successful scene at least another ten times. Your outlook on the situation will change.

4. **Be clear about how you want the event to go and how you want it to end.**
   We tend to be the most nervous at the beginning and the end. If you are clear about these two parts, then you can always fall back on autopilot if you get really nervous. For example, if it is a presentation you are nervous about, write down the beginning and end and practice these two parts the most. That way you will know them to the point of not having to think about them. The point here is to pay particular attention to the areas that make you the most nervous, which is usually the beginning and the end.

5. **Play through the worst-case scenario and then the best-case scenario.**
   People usually believe that by thinking through a worst-case scenario they will become more stressed and afraid. Actually, the solution is to play out the worst-case scenario all the way to the end by continually asking yourself, and then what would happen? Unfortunately, many of us stop mentally

working through this worst-case scenario as soon as we come up against our fear. Instead, play out the scenario completely, as if you are watching a movie. If you were watching a movie, you wouldn't stop the movie as soon as the main character got in trouble, and you wouldn't even assume the character was doomed. You would watch the movie to the end to see what happened. That's what you must do when you envision your worst-case scenario. Most of the time you will simply discover that you are right back where you started. In some cases, the worst-case scenario exercise can help you learn from potential mistakes. Suppose you are afraid to ask for a raise. Well, if you go ahead and ask — despite your fear — the answer may still be no. But in that process, you may receive some helpful feedback. At the very least, you now know where you stand so you can make some decisions about your future.

The point here is that parts of your worst-case scenario may come true when you face a fear. But chances are you will have learned something from the experience, and you may even be better off than you were before.

If your worst-case scenario has you ending up in the gutter, homeless, or in jail, don't worry. Those consequences are most likely *not* the result of one conversation or one event not going well. More likely, that would require a series of bad choices. In life, one thing usually doesn't hurt us that badly — it's the continued procession of bad choices. Eating fast food once in a while won't make you overweight. But, if you eat fast food every single day, you may need new clothes pretty quickly.

After you have played through the worst-case scenario, play out the best-case scenario and notice how you feel. There is a lot more room for positive thought when we clear out the negative doom and gloom. If you are like most people who have gone through this exercise, you will find yourself more willing to tackle the fear, all because you have a clearer picture of possible outcomes. Now you can prepare for them!

Michael Pritchard said, "Fear is the darkroom where negatives are developed." Don't stop yourself from doing and saying things you want and need to do. Fear is like an alarm. You decide how you want to respond to it. You can take action whether or not you are afraid. Fear can't stop you — only *you* can stop you.

Remove Labels and Stereotypes Put on You

UNFORTUNATELY, MANY PEOPLE talk to each other with the labeling method of communication. This happens when someone tailors their communication to a person based on how they categorize or stereotype that person. People use many factors, including race, gender, sexual orientation, age, job, department, organizational level, accent, hearsay information, living location, and technical ability — all to label others. The list is almost endless. Once someone labels a person, they often stop communicating with the person as an individual and instead communicate through that perceived label.

You may think you never label others — and certainly not by race or gender! But what about by job title, appearance, word choice, or alma mater?

Have you ever said or heard anything like this?

- "Oh, he's just a techie. You know how those geeks are. Why can't they just speak plainly?"

- "Those non-technical people, why do we always have to spell everything out for them? What kind of education did they receive anyway?"

- "New college grads. They think they know everything and should own the place. Don't they appreciate experience and tenure?"

- "Those Baby Boomers — all they think about is retirement. They are so stuck in their ways, they will never change."

- "Those people in resources, they all say the same thing. There's no sense even asking for anything — you know what they are going to say."

- "Women... they just get all emotional..."

- "Typical man... doesn't have a clue..."

The fact is that most people *do* label others in some way. But what do you do when you are being wrongly labeled, categorized, or stereotyped? What if you are the one being labeled as a difficult person to work with or as a poor performer? How about when you are new to a situation, and someone has labeled or judged you simply because of the organization or group you are part of? What do you do? How can you stop it?

THE LABEL ENDER™

It's upsetting to find out that you've been labeled or stereotyped, but following this four-step process, the Label Ender™, can help remove that unwanted label.

1. **Bring the label out into the open.**

   Just because no one mentions the label doesn't mean it isn't there. Most people will be uncomfortable admitting they have labeled or categorized you. By bringing it up, you can address the issue and deal with it. Rest assured, if you don't bring up the issue, no one else will either. Just make sure you bring it up as a concern, not an accusation. This gives people permission to address and talk about it without putting them on the defensive. For example, you might say, "I am concerned that you have labeled me as someone who is difficult to work with."

2. **Educate others about what is different this time.**

   Let them know why the label is incorrect. If it used to be correct, let them know what is different now. People often *say* that things have changed, that things are going to be different, so the key here is to give specifics about what has changed. If you have a reputation for being difficult to work with, let them know what has changed and what you have learned. Or tell people how you will approach things or what you are now aware of. Apologizing and admitting a mistake can go a long way in this situation. Your apology may help others let go of the past and be open to accepting your changed behavior. You can also apologize on behalf of your organization, if you need to.

3. **Request the opportunity for a fresh start.**

   Admit things won't be perfect, but ask for a second chance. The human mind tends to only remember the information that confirms an existing opinion. For example, if someone labels you as a poor job performer, they will look for and notice times that you make mistakes. If you do something that is good, they will rationalize that you were lucky. Request a fresh start. They may not concede, but your request will make them more likely to look for and notice improvements.

4. **Do what you say you will do and produce desired results.**

   Do the best job you can. Start building a new "resume" filled with successes. Show them that the fresh start they have given you is well deserved. There are tips that are important to the success of this fourth step. First, make sure you manage expectations at the start. If you can't do something, say so. Second, periodically schedule meetings with the person who has labeled you to inform them about the project status and to keep them in the loop. This also gives you a chance to be your own PR agent and let them know of your successes. Third, when mistakes happen (which they sometimes do), don't wait for them to notice; proactively and immediately address the error with the person. Apologize and explain what is going to be different, and then keep your word and produce desired results. For example, let's say you just started working for an organization with performance issues, and you replaced a person who did a poor job of customer service. If you apply the Label Ender Process™, this is how a conversation with the customer might go.

   "Mr. Customer, I want you to know that I am concerned that you might judge me because of the performance of my predecessor. On behalf of my organization, I am sorry. I also want you to know that we have changed some internal processes to ensure that we give you top-notch service." Go into detail about exactly what is different (new processes, changed personnel, or how you are different than your predecessor). After discussing all of this, say, "I ask you to give me a fresh start. I guarantee that you will see a difference." Then, do what you say and produce the desired results.

The important thing is to do the four steps. Proactively bring up the label as a concern, educate the other person about what is going to be different, request a fresh start, and produce the desired results.

You can't make someone think differently, but you can change how you respond to them, which in turn can change their perception of you. The key is to do your part.

Listen for
the Real Message

THE MOST TERRIFIC woman I know is my mother. Her advice over the years has helped me avoid many problems. As embarrassing as this is to admit, I missed out on many years of my mom's wonderful advice. Why? Because I was missing the real message behind her words.

My mother, by her own admission, can be somewhat negative. If I say things are going great, she might ask, "But are you prepared for the future?" Even though I run my own business, she reminds me almost every year that April 15 is tax day. There are many things I am likely to forget, but tax day is not one of them. If there is a possible negative outcome to any situation, my mother can usually predict it and advise me accordingly.

Unfortunately, for years I took her words as a form of disrespect. I thought her negativity and her tendency to play devil's advocate were signs that she thought I was incapable of doing things right and that she had little faith in my business acumen or my instincts for survival. I reasoned that if she really respected me, she would not be the voice of doom.

Things changed one day when I was attending a seminar. The speaker reminded us not to get caught up in the words people say but to listen for the true message they are trying to convey. At that moment, the light bulb went on. My mother was talking to me in this way because she cared about me, not because she had no faith in me or my skills! Voicing her worries was her way of expressing her love and protectiveness for me; it was not a form of disrespect. Suddenly, I got it.

I vowed from that moment forward to hear the real message my mom was trying to communicate and to be patient with her. She may use words that sound negative, but now I view her worries and warnings as an expression of love. She is simply trying to contribute and point out things that she perceives as helpful.

Of course, as soon as I really started to listen to my mom, I realized how smart and wise she is. She has subsequently saved me on many occasions by pointing out things I would otherwise have overlooked because of my ceaseless optimism.

Are you missing anyone's real message? A client's? A co-worker's? A friend's?

Let's take a work example. When someone complains to you, do you hear just the complaints, or do you take time to recognize the impetus behind the complaints? Perhaps the complainer is not actually trying to be difficult. Perhaps the complainer just wants to be noticed and appreciated for the work they are doing. Or perhaps the complainer is dedicated to the job and wants to excel. Maybe the complainer feels frustrated by a lack of resources and may think it is helpful to point out insufficiencies. Some complainers lack the skill or self-confidence to ask for what they really need. They complain, hoping that others will get the hint and provide it.

Complaining clients who are hard to work with can become our best, most-loyal clients *if* we take the time to hear their real message and address their concerns. If our clients truly do not want to make things work, or if they really have given up, they would probably remain silent and quietly end the relationship as soon as possible.

If we are not careful to hear the real messages people are trying to communicate, we will miss them... and possibly miss out on great opportunities as well. Remember, you cannot change what people say, but you can change the way you choose to hear them. So now, when my mom is predicting gloom and doom in my life, I simply smile and say, "Mom, I got it. You love me."

Handling Other People's Negativity

ADDRESSING NEGATIVITY CAN be complex, because negativity and disagreement are often confused. It is helpful to have someone express an opposing view, so flaws can be addressed, but if we try to stamp out *all* negativity, we will give the impression that the only correct opinion is our own. When this happens, some people may stop providing valuable feedback and information.

On the other hand, if not properly handled, negativity can be harmful to a team, department, or organization. Negativity is like a weed, and if weeds aren't dealt with, they spread. In a group setting, negativity can severely decrease morale, productivity, and effectiveness. The following techniques can help you address negativity in your group.

1. **Acknowledge the person being negative with a sincere and appropriate compliment.**

   Sometimes people are negative, because they don't feel appreciated. In other words, negativity can actually be a cry for attention. Acknowledge the person for something that you appreciate about them and see what happens.

2. **Point out the negativity.**

   Many people don't realize they are being negative. Often, they think they are simply being honest and helpful. Point out how they are coming across and the effect their words and attitude are having on the group. If they rarely say anything positive or offer potential solutions, let them know that as well. If this person does not agree with your perspective, ask them to keep track of how many criticisms versus solutions they offer in a week. Or, you could keep track. This depends on your position. Obviously, if you are the person's manager, you have the authority and responsibility to proactively resolve the situation, and others on the team probably want you to do so.

3. **Facilitate a solution.**

   Helping this person come up with a solution is especially important when you are in a meeting. The key part of this strategy is to ask, "What would you suggest?" It is difficult for someone to continue to be negative when you consistently ask, "What would you suggest?" This takes the focus off of the past and makes the discussion more positive and solution-focused.

4. **Coach them if they are willing to look at things in a different way.**

   Someone who is negative often wants to change but doesn't know how. If this is the case, you can coach them. But first, you must gauge their degree of openness. Start by asking the person if they are open to the possibility of seeing the situation differently. You may even ask if they are open to the possibility that they may be wrong. If they indicate they are not open, you may want to move on and not waste your time. Interestingly enough, sometimes by merely asking that question, the person examines their behavior and becomes open to other points of view. If they are open, then give them your perspective and advice. If they are willing, then make sure your coaching provides tangible, specific actions and accountability, if they so choose.

5. **Allow them to say their piece and then move on.**

   This technique is especially important in a meeting when the person is not open to another point of view. Remember that other people usually want you to move on; most of us aren't interested in getting caught up in a negativity battle. After something negative is said, move on by saying something like, "For the sake of time, let's move on. Our next point is..." Use this technique selectively. If you just move on, you run the risk of the person tuning you out and possibly becoming disruptive for the remainder of the meeting.

6. **Choose to avoid people who are negative.**

   Choose to spend time with people who have attitudes you admire. It is amazing how often people allow themselves to be around people with lousy attitudes. If you cannot control who surrounds you, try to limit the time you spend with them. For example, if a co-worker starts complaining about the work environment or another person, politely excuse yourself from the conversation.

While an opposing point of view can be helpful, persistent negativity never is. Constant negativity can affect our emotions and waste our time. But now you have the steps to take action. The question is, what are you going to do about it? (See "Eliminate Complaining" in real-world solution 6.)

Forgive and Be Free

FORGIVENESS IS A gift you give yourself. When someone says, "I am not going to forgive that person. I am not going to let them get away with that," they think they are punishing the other person. In reality they are only punishing themselves. When we forgive someone, it has nothing to do with letting the person off the hook, forgetting what that person did, or even permitting that person to remain in your life. Forgiveness is a gift you give yourself so you can move forward in your life. It is a choice — an act of courage that allows you to grow stronger and wiser.

How often do you meet people who haven't forgiven someone? Have you ever met someone who seems stuck in the past? Someone who is unable or unwilling to move forward? They are paying the price of not forgiving.

If you think a lack of forgiveness isn't costly, examine two categories of costs: lost time and damage to other relationships.

Here are a few questions to consider:

- How much time do I spend thinking about this issue?

- Has it become my primary focus?

- Am I unable to concentrate on other things and/or people because I am preoccupied?

- Do I ramble on about this issue to the point where people are tired of hearing it?

- Do I lose sleep because I am thinking about it?

- Am I allowing this issue to bleed into and affect my other relationships?

- Does my unwillingness to forgive cause me to punish other people by being overly sensitive, protective, suspicious, or unwilling to trust?

- Have I stopped taking chances because I live in fear that this situation will happen again?

A lack of forgiveness is burdensome and distracting. It saps our energy and joy and can become a source of constant stress. If you are living without forgiving, it is time to get free.

SEVEN STEPS TO FORGIVENESS FREEDOM™

By following the Seven Steps to Forgiveness Freedom™, you can free yourself from the past and empower yourself to produce amazing results in the present in order to accomplish your dreams in the future.

Here's the key: *You must complete each step in this process exactly the way it is described. No variation.* You might be tempted to alter, rush through, or even skip a step. If you do, this exercise will not produce the results you want. Following these steps can change your life forever. It has freed others who have suffered for years, and it can free you too.

1. Brainstorm a list of all your thoughts about the situation that requires forgiveness. These thoughts may sound like this: "People can't be trusted;" "Men (or women) are jerks;" or "My boss is only out for himself." Write down everything that comes to mind. Make sure you work on this list on at least *three* separate occasions. Approaching the list several different times will ensure you capture and hopefully exhaust all of your thoughts.

2. Now brainstorm (in writing) a list of empowering lessons you could learn from this situation. In other words, write down all the potential lessons you can think of that could produce a positive difference in your life. I'm not saying that you have to be glad you went through this tough situation. But since you cannot change the past, what lessons could you choose to learn from it to make a significant and positive difference in your life? Perhaps you will learn to stand up for yourself, set better priorities, or ask for what you really want in life. Like the first step, please make sure you work on this list at least on *three* separate occasions to exhaust all of your thoughts.

3. From the list in step two, choose three lessons that would make a significant and positive difference in your life.

4. Decide upon and schedule at least one action (per lesson learned) that you are going to take within the next two weeks. These actions should be ones that will start you on your journey to really learn and grow (mentally, physically, and emotionally) from each of these designated lessons. The actions chosen may lead to other actions and help build momentum, so that you can leave the past where it belongs — behind you.

Example 1: After receiving constructive criticism from your supervisor regarding your performance, establish a plan with him or her to correct your performance. You could also commit to writing out your own goals, priorities, and expectations, showing your boss for approval. In addition, you could schedule regular meetings with your boss to review your goals and make sure he or she is aware of your accomplishments.

Example 2: If someone has violated your trust, commit to reading self-improvement books, seeing a therapist, and/or taking a course on relationships. This may help you determine what you may or may not have done to contribute to the problem or show you signs that you may have missed. You could also have a direct conversation with the person who violated your trust. Own up to the fact that holding on to the past has hurt you. Then, tell the person you forgive them — if that is the case. This does not require you to become friends or spend time with this person in the future. Remember, this is not about forgetting; it is about forgiving. Any of these actions can give you confidence that the next relationship will not be a repeat of or a reaction to the past. Instead, it could be your best relationship ever, because you have learned, grown, and benefited from your past.

5. Tell someone the actions you have chosen to take and your deadline for taking them. Ask that person to hold you accountable and create a consequence for not following through. For example, tell the person that you'll give them a hundred dollars for every action you don't take on time.

6. Choose a celebration for each action taken. For example, treat yourself to a dinner of your choice. Again, ask someone to hold you accountable. The point here is to acknowledge, appreciate, and reward yourself for moving forward in your life. This will also help build momentum to continue to take other actions that will culminate in a significant difference in your life.

7. Finally, decide on a challenging, powerful goal that compels and inspires you to leave the past behind. For example, if someone violated your trust in a personal relationship, commit to being in a serious, healthy relationship by a specific date.

If you ever doubt your ability to forgive someone, remember Nelson Mandela. Many would say he was entitled to harbor resentment and animosity toward the people who imprisoned him for twenty-seven years. He did not. He forgave them, and amazingly many of those who held him prisoner participated in his inauguration as the president of South Africa. By freely forgiving, Nelson Mandela not only helped himself, he helped an entire nation heal and move forward.

If Nelson Mandela can forgive people for wrongly imprisoning him, I think we can all forgive someone if we so choose. Choose to give yourself the gift of forgiveness. Free yourself from the past, so that you can live freely in the future and have the life you deserve!

Develop a
Positive State of Mind

IN TODAY'S WORK world, many organizations are under-resourced and understaffed; therefore, people are overworked. Managing our careers and remaining motivated under that sort of stress can be challenging. So, how can we stay focused and handle all the challenges that affect our attitude, morale, and effectiveness? The answer is to have an Ownership Attitude.

I used to have a television show, during which I interviewed successful people. I found that one of the defining characteristics to success is an Ownership Attitude. When this attitude is adopted, we understand that we are in full control of ourselves and that no one else is responsible or to blame for our attitude. We accept responsibility for our thoughts, opinions, assumptions, and conclusions. We *choose* to think and act a certain way. We may not be able to control the circumstances around us, but we *can* control how we respond to those circumstances.

This may seem simple and obvious, but have you ever caught yourself or someone else saying things like this?

- *They* pressured me.
- *They* made me say it.
- *They* made me do it.
- *They* made me upset.
- *They* ruined my day.

We often say these things while under stress, but they do not make logical sense. When we say such things, we are saying *others* control us. Obviously, this is not the truth. *We* are in control of ourselves. The only way that someone can ever control us is if we *allow* them to do so.

In the short run, we may feel better when we blame someone else, but it is only a matter of time before the misery returns. Why? Because when we blame others, we relinquish our control of the situation. We are saying that the other person is responsible, and we have to wait for them to do something about the situation. Furthermore, blaming others can blind us to the ways in which we may be contributing to a difficult situation.

When we are sitting in traffic getting mad, who is responsible? We are! We cannot control the traffic, but we can control our response to it. If someone cuts us off and we go home with a miserable attitude and let the rest of the night be ruined, whose fault is it? Ours. The driver who cut us off isn't even thinking about us. I once had a seminar participant challenge me about this. He said, "You don't understand. If someone cuts me off, they make me chase them down."

After people laughed, I said, "Isn't that interesting? You are allowing the other driver to have complete emotional control over you." The participant admitted that he had never thought of it that way. Of course, the truth is that no one can make you do anything.

The next time you find yourself choosing to surrender control of your attitude, implement the Three-Step Emotional Turnaround Solution™.

1. **Acknowledge your own emotion.**

   When you are upset, acknowledge the emotion you are feeling by saying something like, "I am upset/stressed/annoyed," or whatever. Avoid saying to yourself, "Calm down," or "Don't get upset," or "Don't worry." Don't invalidate your feelings. Acknowledging your emotions allows them to dissipate. Someone once said, "What you resists, persists."

2. **Analyze the situation.**

   Instead of asking, "Why do they do this to me?" ask, "Why am I allowing this person or situation to bother me?" This is far more effective and helpful. The answer to the question may reveal a persistent fear or insecurity. For instance, if you question yourself because you find yourself getting upset with a co-worker who is not performing up to standards, you may discover that you're afraid their performance will have a negative effect on your ability to get your job done. And that, in turn, may have a negative effect on your career. Understanding *why* we become so emotional often reveals more about ourselves than the other person or situation.

3. **Take action.**

   Ask yourself, "What am I going to do about it?" Letting it go can also be a solution — as long as we really *do* stop complaining about it and move on. For most of us, taking some sort of action is key. Otherwise, nothing will change and the situation will only grow worse. So if you find yourself complaining, stop and consider what you're willing to do about the situation. You can also consider what lessons you have learned or can learn that will allow you to grow, benefit, and prevent the difficulty in the future.

USING THE THREE-STEP EMOTIONAL TURNAROUND SOLUTION™

Here's an example. Suppose you are sitting in a traffic jam and you are starting to become upset. First, acknowledge your emotions. Don't tell yourself to calm down. Second, analyze the situation by asking yourself, *Why am I allowing this to get me so upset?* Maybe you're upset because you're going to be late. Third, ask yourself, *What am I willing to do about this? What lessons can I learn from the situation that will allow me to grow, benefit, and prevent this situation in the future?* In this case, the answer might be to leave fifteen minutes earlier and get some books on tape. This way, you can enjoy the ride and arrive at work in a good frame of mind.

By following and implementing the Three-Step Emotional Turnaround Solution™, you can empower yourself to transform virtually any situation.

NINE TIPS FOR AN OWNERSHIP ATTITUDE

1. **Let people know that you are aware of your attitude and ask for their support.**
   People can be incredibly understanding, compassionate, encouraging, and helpful when you are willing to ask for help. Some people may be skeptical (which may be an appropriate response), but don't let that deter you. Apologize, and ask them to be supportive and encouraging.

People tend to be inspired and honored when you want their help.

2. **Be clear about your sense of purpose — where you are going and why it is important to you.**
A strong sense of purpose and direction will help you not get hung up on small, insignificant things. You are more likely to weather the bumps when you know your destination.

3. **Control your focus.**
The difference between focusing on what is wrong versus focusing on what is right can make an amazing difference in our attitude — and the attitude of the people around us. Don't ignore reality, but be sure to focus on what is going well, what you appreciate, and what you are thankful for. Take ten minutes daily (preferably in the morning) to go for a walk alone and say out loud all the things you appreciate. Watch your attitude — and the attitude of those around you — change.

4. **Examine and change your self-talk.**
I often see people who want to change their perspective on things, yet continually talk about how much they hate something. If we continually tell ourselves something, we tend to focus on that one thing almost exclusively. The key is to have powerful, empowering self-talk. If you find it is hard to say positive and empowering things, try sharing out loud all your fears and concerns first. This may feel odd, but try it. Think of it as dumping out all the garbage. You may want to do this alone — in your car on the way to work for a tough meeting or in your office before you have to make a stressful call. You'll know when you are done sharing the bulk of

your concerns and fears, because you will begin to feel a sense of relief. Once you get the concerns and fears out, start verbalizing empowering and positive statements. Try saying, "Things are going to go great." Or you could say, "Everyday I do what it takes to enjoy and love my life." Or how about, "I am so grateful to have wonderful people in my life." The point here is to examine and change your self-talk to empower you every day.

5. **Give people the benefit of the doubt — we don't know what we don't know.**
   The facts are the facts, but the meaning you attach to those facts is yours. For example, if someone did not call you back, the fact is that they did not call you back. You don't know why they did not call you back. Maybe they never received your message; maybe they were too embarrassed to call, since they did not do what they said they would do; or maybe they are out sick. Or let's say someone snaps at you. You don't necessarily know *why* they snapped at you. Maybe it has nothing to do with you. Maybe they are under pressure from things happening at home or other projects that you are unaware of. I am not saying that their behavior is appropriate, but I am saying you don't necessarily know the reason for it. Extend the benefit of the doubt.

6. **Choose to spend your time with people who have the attitude you would like to have.**
   If you want to get better at tennis, you play with people who are better than you. In the same way, you should spend time with people you admire and want to be like. It is a lot easier to develop a healthy mindset around people who have one. Just as parents are concerned about who their kids hang out

with, so you should be concerned with the group you hang out with.

7. **Choose to read things that provide information about and examples of the way you want to think and the attitude you want to have.**
   If your reading choices are books and articles about how difficult or challenging the relationship between men and women can be, is it any wonder you think the opposite gender is difficult to deal with? Instead, choose what you read carefully. Books and articles are food for your mind — make sure your reading material isn't junk food.

8. **When you're thinking negatively or blaming others — stop, take a five-minute break, close your eyes, and let go of your upsetting attitude.**
   If it helps to have a visual image, imagine letting all the negativity and blaming thoughts out of a cage as you exhale.

9. **People who acknowledge others tend to have great attitudes.**
   How often do you acknowledge others? When we acknowledge someone, we have to think positively. The more we acknowledge others, the more positive moments we have. Over time, we feel better about ourselves and those around us.

Taking ownership of your attitude will empower you to feel better about yourself, your surroundings, and others, which can make all the difference in the world.

REAL-WORLD
SOLUTION

The Key to Staying Engaged in Conversations

RECENTLY, I RECEIVED a call from a woman who wanted advice on why she was not getting job offers. She had been to fifteen interviews and felt that during the interviews she became unfocused and inadequately answered the interview questions. When asked if she brought a pad and pencil to the interview, she was dumbfounded. It never occurred to her that the key to listening and focusing during a conversation was to take notes!

Even people who know this still don't do it. Why? Because they feel awkward and uncomfortable — or worse, they think others will feel awkward and uncomfortable. So what can you do? Be upfront. Tell people why you are taking notes. Your explanation should eliminate any tension or curiosity. Remind the other party that the notes will benefit all of the parties involved in the conversation.

Here are four reasons why notes are beneficial.

1. **Memory**

   Using notes during a discussion ensures the parties involved will address every issue that needs to be covered. This is not only a benefit for ourselves, but for the others in the discussion. Have you ever walked out of a discussion without mentioning an important topic? Unfortunately, if we attempt to resume the conversation at a later time, we might be labeled as high maintenance or as a complainer who is never done with an issue. Or, we may appear disorganized. On the other hand, if we don't bring it up, the issue lingers and gets worse. This is stressful, costly, and wastes valuable time. By bringing notes and recording key points, we ensure all topics are covered and all issues are thoroughly resolved.

2. **Ability to listen**

   Bringing and taking notes will allow us to listen to others in the discussion, especially if we are interrupted. Many of us try to cope with interrupters by asking them not to interrupt, because we are afraid that we might forget where we were or what we were going to say. This may be acceptable on occasion, but it can lead to communication breakdowns. Here's why. If we say something the other person disagrees with and they cannot interrupt and speak their mind in response, they will tune us out. They simply will stop listening, dwelling only on the point they want to make, and wait for their turn to speak. Notes allow us to stay on track, fully listen, and not worry about where we were when we were interrupted. When the interrupter has finished commenting, we can simply go back to the notes. Taking notes during a conversation is also important; it helps us not to interrupt, especially when the other person is long-winded or brings up points we disagree with. This way, when they are done, we can revisit and address our points, if necessary.

3. Focus

Notes can prevent a conversation from wandering and keep the discussion focused on its intended purpose. This is especially important when highly charged issues are being discussed. How many times have we walked away from an all over the place conversation or a meeting and thought, "What was that all about? We did not accomplish anything." No one wants to waste time. By bringing notes, we can keep the conversation on track and communicate our thoughts in a straightforward manner. This will benefit everyone involved and helps ensure our encounters are meaningful and successful.

4. Importance

Bringing notes demonstrates to the other person that the conversation or meeting is important. Your preparation demonstrates that you appreciate their time. Bringing notes will make the other parties feel respected and appreciated. As a result, they will be more likely to participate.

Using notes will enhance your ability to communicate, listen, and stay focused. People in your life will soon begin to understand that a conversation with you is useful, productive, and produces results — which is a benefit to everyone!

Deal with Disruptive Behavior

ARE THERE PEOPLE in your life who exhibit negativity or difficult behavior, yet seem unaware of it? Waiting and hoping for things to change won't bring results, but the tips in this chapter may raise their awareness of the behavior and change the situation. These tips can be used in combination with one another, and not all may be applicable to all situations. Furthermore, some of these tips are quite drastic, so be sure to exercise sound judgment. As you use these tips, be careful about your reaction. You need to allow time for the situation to de-escalate and resolve. Remember, big problems were once small problems that developed over time.

One quick note — when I suggest dialogue, people often will say, "Oh, I can't say that." Please don't get hung up on the exact dialogue. Simply use your own words and sincere style to implement the strategy or tip.

Here are six techniques to use when someone is unaware of their disruptive behavior.

1. **Point out the behavior and ask the person what they intend to accomplish with it.**

    For example, you might say, "I notice you are condescending and sarcastic with me. Where are you going with this?" Or you could say, "What is your goal in saying that?" This will cause the other person to stop and think, *What am I doing? What is my intention?* This alone may cause someone to alter their behavior, because people often don't stop and consider the ramifications of their actions. If appropriate, you can tell them that the negative behavior won't achieve their desired outcome. In other words, their behavior does not encourage or inspire you to help them nor work with them. In fact it has the opposite effect.

2. **State the facts and share your emotions.**

    Say something such as, "I've noticed your sarcasm and condescending comments. That hurts my feelings." The key is not to blame them for how you feel. Instead, simply state how you feel.

3. **Make a request and let them know what benefit there is for them.**

    If you want someone to change their behavior, you have to show them the benefit. For example, you might say, "My request is that we do not raise our voices as we discuss this. By not raising our voices, we will be more likely to listen to each other and think through a possible solution that will work for both of us."

4. **Use the turn-around principle.**

   Ask, "What would you do if you were me and someone was doing this to you?" This often serves as a great wake-up call, because people don't often consider how they would feel if they were on the receiving end of their own behavior.

5. **State the name of the behavior and then ask if they want you to use the same behavior on them.**

   This may come across as confrontational, so I would suggest you only use this approach in extreme cases where nothing else has worked and things really need to change. For example, if someone turns projects in late, you could say, "Do you want me to break my word to you and turn things in late? What if I held up the paperwork you expected from me?" Or if someone is always late, you could ask, "Do you want me to start showing up late and keep you waiting?" The key is to make them aware of how much they would dislike this behavior — and its results — if it were to happen to them.

6. **Treat them as they have treated you.**

   This is a radical and severe step that can only be done with certain people in certain situations. This step should only be taken if the other steps have not worked. In fact, if not done well, this step can backfire. To use this technique, first you must warn the person that since things have not changed — despite your feedback and repeated requests — you are now going to treat them as they are treating you. If someone is always late, you then show up *really* late and keep them waiting. If someone has not been honest with you, tell them you are going to lie to them. Lie to them when they don't expect it. When they get upset, share that you feel the same way when they lie to you. Again, this is a risky technique that should only be utilized in certain situations.

Please remember, these techniques are only options and may not be applicable to your situation. The most important thing is to talk to the person and make it clear that you want the behavior to stop. The longer you wait to address the behavior, the worse the situation may get. Be clear and stand your ground. (See "MT. SAMIE" in real-world solution 4.)

Inspire
Excellence in Others

WE ARE ALL leaders in some capacity. We may lead our staff, boss, co-workers, clients, family, and friends. The key is to lead them honestly. The following are seven keys to providing honest, effective leadership — no matter what the situation or whom we are leading. As you read through these keys, honestly rate yourself on a scale of 1 to 10 (1 being the worst and 10 being the best) to determine what area you need to focus on and improve.

1. **Be honest and keep your word.**
   The foundation of all relationships is trust, and the way to establish trust is through honesty. Being honest and keeping your word are key. While it may be tempting to make a lot of promises or to withhold information to avoid upset in the short run, everyone usually loses in the long run. The benefit of trust is priceless for everyone.

2. Paint an optimistic, positive vision for the future.

Look at the great leaders of our time. They do not exude doom, gloom, misery, and heartache. In fact, effective leaders personify optimism and lay out a bright, exciting future. This does not mean that leaders ignore present problems and challenges; it simply means they are realistic about the present and are preparing for a positive, proactive, and optimistic future. It is okay to take people through the valley of issues and problems as long as we show them how we can make it to the mountaintop of success.

3. Take full responsibility.

Ineffective leaders blame external factors for times of difficulty. Effective leaders focus their time and efforts on what they can do about the external factors. After all, we may not be able to control everything that happens to us, but we are always in control of our response. By focusing 100 percent of our energies on what we can control, we can inspire others on our team to do the same.

4. Provide clear goals and an implementation plan.

My friend Jim Ball, author of *DNA Leadership through Goal-Driven Management*, says that crystal-clear goals and a plan to achieve those goals is paramount to success. If we are not sure where we are going, how can we expect anyone to follow us? Have you ever encountered someone who either was not sure what they wanted or couldn't articulate it, yet they wanted you to follow and support them? Have you ever done this? If we want to lead, we must know where we are going and how we will get there — and then ensure that others know how we will get there together.

5. **Clarify expectations.**

People often have a hard time focusing on and prioritizing what needs to be done. As leaders, it is important to be explicit. Remind team members what they are accountable for and what you expect of them. For example, in our office, being honest and keeping your word (doing what we say we are going to do) are non-negotiable expectations. Because these are stated expectations, everyone knows them and operates accordingly. People tend to rise to the level of expectations — they just need to know what those expectations are.

6. **State the benefits for the other person.**

Remember, the universal language we speak is, "What is in it for me?" Make sure people explicitly and implicitly know how your organizational goals, plans, and expectations will benefit them on an individual and personal level. Incidentally, this is why many organizations' vision or mission statements don't have the desired impact on employees. Employees often don't see the benefit to them. Great leaders show how everyone impacts the bottom line and makes a difference as well as how everyone will reap the rewards by achieving goals.

7. **Appreciate the people around you.**

One of the biggest complaints among employees is lack of appreciation. It is astonishing when you think about it, because appreciation does not necessarily cost anything, and yet it can make a huge difference. After all, I have yet to hear of someone who left an organization (or a marriage for that matter) because he or she was over appreciated. Yet people leave situations all the time because they don't feel appreciated. So, acknowledge and appreciate your team and organization members. We all want to know that we make a difference.

Now that you have rated yourself, pick the lowest score and share those scores with five people and ask them for advice. Then choose three specific actions that you will perform based on this advice. Ask someone to hold you accountable — and do what you said you would do. By making use of these seven keys, you can successfully lead others and make a significant difference in the lives of many. (See the "Law of Reflection" in real-world solution 14 and "MT. SAMIE" in real-world solution 4.)

Get Others to Share Their Ideas

IN TODAY'S INCREDIBLY competitive work world, it is imperative to tap into the resources, ideas, and knowledge of the people around us. Research indicates that many of the greatest ideas do not come from the headquarters of an organization, but from the front lines. Staff on the front lines are the closest to the problems, issues, and challenges any organization faces. These are the people who know how things really work. Without this information and perspective, organizations can become stale, lose their competitive edge, and ultimately become extinct.

Are the people around you sharing their thoughts, ideas, and perspectives? Have you created an environment in which people feel safe to do so? After a problem is uncovered, do you find yourself thinking, *if only I had known*? That may be a sign that the environment you've created is not safe enough.

Sometimes we fool ourselves into thinking that we are hearing most of the ideas and opportunities around us. But just consider how often you or others you know have failed to express ideas, rationalizing that no one cares or that it won't do any good. So it is only logical to consider that others might be doing this with you as well. Unfortunately, sometimes we condition people *not* to share their ideas with us.

We tell people we want to hear their ideas and opportunities, but when they actually do, we may debate them or not take the time to really listen. Consequently, the next time we ask for feedback and ideas, that person probably won't be willing to share, because they anticipate another negative response.

Organizations as a whole can discourage people from sharing their ideas. For example, sometimes organizations give employee surveys and then don't provide feedback on those surveys for months, if at all. In some cases, no information is provided about specific actions the organization will take to make improvements. Thus, employees rightly conclude that sharing feedback and ideas will do no good — that it's a waste of their time.

Here are some ideas that you can implement to change this perception. While these keys may seem basic, they're often neglected. Please read each one in detail, rate yourself, and ask yourself how you can improve your rating.

1. **Ask people for their ideas.**

   This seems obvious, but employees often complain that no one asks them — and they are too timid to offer. The key is to constantly ask people for their ideas — and ask them in a variety of settings. Ask people in official meetings, in ad hoc and random meetings, and in one-on-one conversations. Some people are more comfortable in one setting versus another. If you keep asking them in different ways and in different situations, eventually they will share. Their ideas may lead to new opportunities for the organization. And if employees feel their ideas have made a difference, they will be more likely to offer new ideas without you having to ask. Some organizations even set goals and create rewards for ideas. If you do this, make sure it is for quantity of ideas, not quality. Because through quantity, you usually will get quality. Plus, you may hear some crazy, radical ideas. And as history has shown, those radical ideas may just be groundbreaking.

2. **Appreciate *all* ideas.**
   Take all ideas seriously, regardless of what you're thinking and feeling. Don't dismiss any idea or quickly justify why something will not work. Ideas that seem crazy at first could turn out to be golden. Even though most of the ideas may not be useable, always be careful with your response. Watch your facial gestures, body language, tone of voice, and words. All responses should be open and appreciative. Clearly convey how much you value the input. Appreciating people for sharing ideas sends the message that you want them to keep coming.

3. **Credit the creator of the idea.**
   Many participants in my seminars have experienced a co-worker stealing an idea and taking the credit. They share how upsetting and disillusioning that is. Make sure you give credit to the originator of the idea when you put it to use — even if the idea has evolved or you have altered it slightly. This is critical for maintaining trust and creativity in an organization. It encourages the free flow of ideas, because it lets people know that sharing ideas and opportunities is not

a waste of time. Instead, people will see that their ideas are a valuable resource — a resource that will be acknowledged and rewarded. Make sure you understand how the originator wants to be credited. Some people prefer public praise; some prefer private acknowledgement. Either way, make sure credit is given to the originator as soon as possible.

So, how do you rate? Hopefully you can see ways to improve and better solicit ideas and opportunities within your organization. Getting people to share their ideas openly and honestly is a process that can always be improved. When we create an environment where people want to share their ideas, we all reap the rewards! (See "Train and Condition Results Method" in real-world solution 18.)

REAL-WORLD
SOLUTION

Keep Others Focused in Turbulent Times

PEOPLE BECOME STRESSED and unfocused for all sorts of reasons — organizational changes, job changes, personal issues, and even world events. When this happens, how do you keep others focused and at the same time support them? Being open with them about what needs to be accomplished and allowing them to be honest with you is the key. So, how do you do that?

Here are four key steps.

1. **Allow others to express their emotions.**
   Expressing emotion is a great way for people to begin to free themselves from their built-up feelings — especially stress, worry, fear, and anxiety. Unfortunately, many people encourage others not to express emotion by saying such things as: "Check your emotions at the door," or "Don't show emotion," or "Keep your feelings inside." This is similar to putting

a lid on a pot of boiling water. Eventually it will boil over, and when it does, it will be a mess. The more we allow others to express their emotions in an appropriate way, the more likely it is that their emotions will dissipate. In this way, they will be able to refocus on what needs to be accomplished.

2. **Acknowledge other people's emotions.**
Once someone expresses an emotion, acknowledge it. We can do so by saying something like, "I understand you are upset" (or stressed or annoyed). Try to avoid saying something like, "I understand you are upset, BUT…" The *but* makes someone feel invalidated. Saying, "Don't get upset" or "Don't worry" has the same effect. In fact, when we tell someone to "not feel" a certain way, it can have the opposite effect and make them even more emotional, because they then feel invalidated. Instead, the more we acknowledge another person's emotions, the more likely it is that their emotions will be diffused, and then we can begin to help them address the issue.

3. **Ask how you can support them.**
Often people know what they need to feel supported. Problems occur when we don't ask what they need or, worse, when we give them advice they have not asked for. If you do ask how to assist or support someone and they say they don't know, they often mean, "I am afraid to ask you for help." If that happens, ask the question again and assure the person you really want to help. When they tell you what they need, work out an agreement that is suitable for both of you. The key is to be proactive and to ask them first. You may be surprised to find out that all they wanted you to do was to listen.

4. Constantly remind them of the big picture and goals.
This crucial step helps by putting the immediate problem in context, so they can re-focus. When people are upset, they tend to overly concentrate on the present and forget their future goals. By reminding others what they are working toward and where they are going, they will be more likely to move beyond the present and achieve what they originally set out to accomplish.

There are many strategies that can be used to help people cope and focus during challenging times. The key is to be upfront and allow the person to discuss the situation, acknowledge that it is okay to feel what they feel, develop a support plan that works for both parties, and remind them of the big picture. This will allow you to get back to the business at hand. (See "Eliminate Complaining" in real-world solution 6 and "Discover What Others *Really* Want" in real-world solution 16.)

Rebuild Broken Trust

THE FUNDAMENTAL BUILDING block of any relationship — business or personal — is trust. What do you do if someone has broken your trust or you have broken theirs? You can make a significant difference with some simple steps.

If someone has broken your trust, there is usually a fear that the trust will be broken again. Unfortunately, that is often the case unless these four key steps are taken.

1. **Make sure they feel safe to tell you the truth.**

    Consider how you might have conditioned someone to break your trust. Did you punish someone for telling the truth in the past by becoming defensive or upset? Did you penalize them in some way? Many people would prefer to lie than to deal with that kind of reaction again. If you have conditioned someone to not tell you the truth, it is possible to recondition them. The best initial step is to apologize for your behavior and for creating an environment where they don't feel safe to tell you the truth. Apologies go a long way to re-building trust. Then ask, "What can I do in the future to make you feel safe, so I can be assured that you will tell me the truth?" Based on their response, decide on an agreeable plan with specific actions you will perform to establish an environment in which they will feel safe to tell you the truth.

2. **Ask the person, "What is going to be different from this point forward so that I know I will be able to trust you?"**
   If they answer the question by using vague language about unspecific actions, chances are good the trust is going to be broken and the undesired behavior will occur again. Lines such as, "Well, I have learned my lesson" or "I am going to try harder" or "I am going to be more disciplined" or "I won't do that again" mean it is probably going to happen again. People often have good intentions, but after time has passed and emotions have died down, we tend to revert to our old ways. The past predicts the future, unless we take action to do something specifically different. If you are a manager, it is perfectly appropriate and actually responsible to ask specifically what is going to be different — how they will achieve their goals. If they can't come up with any specifics, you can bank on nothing changing.

3. **Create a consequence ahead of time for what will happen if trust is broken again and things don't change.**
   Let's consider the previous example. When someone is not achieving their goals, you can say, "In the spirit of honesty, I just want you to know that I am going to start documenting any future failures. I have to hold you accountable, just like I

do everyone else, to achieving the established goals." This may sound harsh, but by taking this step, the person knows you mean business. If things don't change, it sets in motion (without any surprises) what you are going to do next. Make sure you are ready to implement the consequence. Otherwise, you will be conditioning that person that you don't mean what you say and that the old behavior is okay.

On the personal front, a friend of mine kept making promises that he was going to make a decision about moving in with his girlfriend. After a while, people around him lost trust that he would ever follow through and make a decision. After making another proclamation, someone suggested that if he did not follow through with his latest deadline, he should dress up like a woman and walk around a department store. When he balked, some people challenged him. They said if he really was going to follow through, he would agree to the consequence. The reason for his resistance was that he knew he probably wouldn't follow through. After consideration, he realized they were right and things weren't going to change. He agreed to the consequence, fulfilled the commitment, and they are now happily married.

Sometimes a challenge allows us to see the real issues more clearly. One quick and easy way to gauge how committed someone is to change is to use the $100 test. The $100 test is where you ask the person, "If you do not do what you said, will you be willing to give me $100?" The answer often reveals whether they are serious about changing. You may even want to ask for $1000 and watch their response.

Another way to implement a consequence is to ask the person what they think should be done if they don't fulfill their promise. I like this strategy, because it gets the other person involved in making sure things change. It also reveals how serious a person really is about changing. You could say, "In the spirit of honesty, I need to know that I can trust that this is really going to change. If you are committed to changing, what will you be willing to do as a consequence if things don't change?" Then allow the person some time to think and respond. If the person gives an easy consequence, you can push and challenge them about it, but you should understand that they are probably not committed to change. If someone really is going to change, they will have no problem making a major commitment with a severe consequence. Why? Because they know the consequence is not going to happen, because they know they are going to keep their promise.

4. **Acknowledge the person if and when things do change.**
   Appreciation lets the other person know that you are aware of their efforts. It also goes a long way to encouraging someone to build their momentum and continue to change.

HAVE YOU BROKEN TRUST?

If you have broken someone's trust, flip the advice around. First, sincerely and immediately apologize. Then tell them specifically what you are going to do differently. To give them confidence that you are really going to change, establish a severe consequence that you will self-impose if things do not change.

One piece of advice — if you do change and the person keeps bringing up the past, it is fair to ask of them, "What needs to happen so that you stop bringing up the past?" Often people are unaware of how frequently they bring up the past, and until you point it out, they do not recognize that things really have changed. Make sure you have really changed before you do this.

Trust is the foundation of any great relationship, at work and at home. Without trust, a relationship is like a car on blocks. It isn't going anywhere... and after a while, it will rust and deteriorate. You can make a difference by taking a few simple steps to put your relationship back on track. You hold the keys.

How to Receive Difficult Feedback

PEOPLE OFTEN DISMISS feedback because they don't like it, don't agree with it, or don't like they way it is delivered. But if we dismiss it, we may be sending a message that we don't want to hear any feedback. People may stop coming to us. And if this happens, we may miss valuable information. Remember, where there is smoke, there is fire. When someone tells us something, others usually have similar thoughts but lack the courage to say something. So it is a good idea to assume that others think the same thing.

It may be painful, but receiving feedback is a key to growth in life. If you think about the times you have grown the most, you may notice that those times came after you received some difficult feedback. After I had been conducting seminars for a year, I had a friend attend an evening speech to give me feedback. When I called to get his feedback, he began by saying, "You know, Steve, I am your friend..." and then for the next hour, he proceeded to rip

the presentation apart. I walked around feeling sorry for myself
for several days. I even thought I might be in the wrong profession. But then I realized that virtually all the feedback he gave me
was about things I could change. I took most of his advice, made
the changes, and the next time I delivered the speech, I was light
years ahead of where I would have been without it.

How do you receive advice, especially when it is difficult to
hear or you don't like the way someone says it? Here are four tips.

1. **Think of yourself as a sponge.**

   Listen, soak in the advice, and try not to respond. You can
   always wring it out and let go of it later. Don't respond verbally or non-verbally; stay receptive. Remember, even if you
   are not happy with the feedback, it is better to know than
   not to know. After all, you can't take action on something
   you don't know about. It is better to receive unfiltered feedback than to have others filter it for you.

2. **Take notes.**

   If you find yourself wanting to debate the issue, remind
   yourself not to interrupt. Instead, write down your thoughts
   as the person is talking. If they ask you what you are writing, be honest and say, "I have some thoughts, but I want to
   really hear what you have to say before I respond, and I
   appreciate you talking to me." People usually have mixed
   feelings while giving feedback. If you interject, they may
   turn off the feedback valve. Again, make them feel safe.
   Take notes to reduce the temptation to interrupt, respond,
   or debate.

3. **Separate the message from the messenger.**

   Don't get hung up on the words. Listen for the true message of what they are trying to convey. Sometimes when people are upset (or just because of the way they are), they do not say things in a way that is easy to hear. For example, they may say it with condescension or they may say it with an attitude. This may tempt you to dismiss what they are saying. Catch yourself. Remember, just because you don't like the way someone says something or the person saying it, does not mean what they are saying is not valid, important, or beneficial.

4. **Look for the gold.**

   It is easy to dismiss feedback when you don't like what is said. The hard part is to take it in, sift through it, and look for the gold. Even if a lot of it is off-target, resist the urge to say, "This is wrong and has no merit." Instead, ask yourself, "How can I benefit and grow from this feedback? What is helpful or useful?"

Think of feedback as a growth pill. You can choose whether to swallow it or not. The difference in your life can be tremendous. (See "Create the Relationship You Want" in real-world solution 18.)

Change a Negative Perception

DO OTHERS PERCEIVE you to be negative? Whether or not that perception is correct, you must do something to change it. After all, it is
hard to have successful relationships when others perceive you
that way. Begin by examining and altering your communication.
Watch what you say and alter how you say it.

Follow this process if you have something to say that might be
perceived to be negative.

1. **Check in with yourself before you say it.**
   Ask yourself, what is my objective here? Why do I want to
   say this? You must be honest with yourself. If you're saying
   something to intentionally hurt someone or get back at them,
   stop yourself. If your intention is to improve a situation or
   relationship or to create a positive result, then say it. Just be

honest and check in with yourself. Remember, the worst lies we tell are the lies we tell ourselves.

2. **State the facts of the situation and then ask an effective question rather than making an allegation.**
For example, "I noticed that I left you a couple of messages and did not hear back from you. Is everything okay with what I sent you?" Be patient and listen to the answer.

3. **Share opinions as concerns, not accusations, and follow up with an effective question.**
Don't make definitive, negative proclamations such as: "This project is never going to be successful," or "This project is going to go over budget," or "We are never going to meet that deadline." Instead you could say, "I am concerned that we might go over budget and miss the deadline. What are your thoughts?" Then be open to that person's feedback. This shifts the conversation to a problem-solving one. People may suggest ideas that will make the project better than it was before. Although you may ultimately be correct, you are not a mind reader and you do not want to sound (or be) self-righteous. The team will not be motivated to produce positive results if they feel you believe the project is already destined to fail. Would you want to be part of a doomed or unsuccessful team?

4. **Follow your potentially negative comment or criticism with a potential solution.**
Even if the other person doesn't agree with or adopt your suggested solution, this shows the person that you are not trying to be a naysayer. Instead, it demonstrates that you are

trying to improve the situation and make things work out successfully. The key is to show that you are committed to being part of the solution.

By using any of these tips, you can start to change how people perceive you. Few people want to be around someone who is negative. We gravitate toward sincerely positive people, especially people who are working hard at changing and improving themselves. As the saying goes, *you attract more flies with honey.* (See "Effectively Deliver Bad News" in real-world solution 5 and "How to Receive Difficult Feedback" in real-world solution 33.)

Preventing Repetitive Mistakes

ALBERT EINSTEIN REPORTEDLY said, "The definition of insanity is doing the same thing over and over again and expecting different results." People tend to do exactly that. When they don't like something, they fall back on the same old strategies that have not worked in the past, hoping things will be different this time. Of course, they usually get the same lackluster results and wonder why.

A friend asked for advice about a man she was dating. She told me she liked him but that he wanted her to meet his elderly parents. She was concerned about meeting his parents this early in their relationship. She stated that she liked to take things slowly and wanted to be extremely cautious. I said, "Given what has happened in your past relationships, do you think taking things slowly and being extremely cautious has worked for you?"

She paused, thought a moment, and responded, "I will go meet his parents this weekend." Suddenly it became clear to her that her relationship style was not necessarily working for her. She realized that she took things slowly and cautiously because, in fact, she didn't trust people. By looking into the past and asking herself how successful she has been with her cautiousness, she was able to see that it was not producing the results she wanted. This enabled her to realize that instead of being extra cautious — or going to the other extreme of rushing into a relationship — she should let the other person know about her challenges in trusting people and ask for help. This empowers the other person as a partner to help her find a solution that works for both of them.

After years of working with people, I truly believe that many people are not honest with themselves about how habitual their problem-solving methods are. If they really stand back, self-observe, and become truly aware, they can think about how successful — or unsuccessful — those methods have been for them.

If you are having issues or challenges, honestly look at your methods for trying to resolve them. If they are not producing the results you want, try something different. You may not have all the answers, or you may not know the right answer. But by trying something different, at least you have a chance of breaking through and solving the issue you are wrestling with.

Consider this: there are currently more than six billion people in the world. Add to that the billions of people who have lived before us. With all of those individuals living their lives, the chances are great that *someone* has experienced exactly what we are experiencing and has found a solution. The trick is to find the answer.

It is arrogant and egotistical to say and believe that we have tried everything. The truth is that we may have tried everything we can think of, but we have certainly not tried everything there is to try. Someone out there has probably experienced our problem, has been in an identical or nearly identical situation, and has found the answer. Chances are great that someone out there has a co-worker, boss, husband, wife, child, or relative who has experienced a very similar problem and found a resolution.

This may be hard to see when you're examining your own life, but think about how often you have watched friends or co-workers ignore an obvious solution. They live in the world called "nothing can help me." No matter what you suggest, they reject everything. So, when you feel stuck and don't see any answers, take a look at the bigger picture. If you *believe* there is an answer out there, you will most likely find one. Belief drives actions; actions don't drive beliefs. People often say, "I'll believe it when I see it." The problem is they can't see it, if they don't believe it.

What if you ran your life by the motto: failure is not an option. How determined would you be to find and implement the answer you're looking for? What if there was a million dollars riding on it? How likely would you be to find the answer?

Here is an easy tip to help you find the answers for just about any situation — simply ask ten people for advice. If they don't have the answer, they probably know someone who does. When you receive the advice, be open, receptive, and truly listen to what they have to say.

Sometimes people say that there may be answers out there but that they don't have much control over the situation. That may be so, but you can concentrate on the part you *can* control and see what happens. You may only control 5 percent of the situation, but that can make all the difference. After all, even someone in a kayak with limited control can navigate water rapids successfully.

So, if you are committed to changing a situation, stop doing things that don't work. And when you're tempted to think you have tried everything, remember you haven't. Don't allow failure to be an option — and don't let yourself give up. The odds are someone in the world has gone through the same experience and figured out the answer. Go find it!

11 Questions to Uncover Communication Problems

ALL YOU HAVE to do is turn on the news to see how a lack of honest communication is affecting the workplace as well as everyday relationships we have with one another. In fact, it seems these problems are very common. Therefore, honest, effective communication is even more critical to teamwork, productivity, and profitability and an organization's lifelong success than ever before.

People at all levels of an organization must be willing to honestly share the information, ideas, and opportunities that come up on a daily basis. This honest communication must also be done in a time-sensitive manner, because things change so quickly in today's world. If an organization does not receive critical information in time, it can cost them millions or even billions of dollars. Why? Because problems need to be caught and resolved when they are small, and no organization can afford to miss key opportunities.

People make better decisions when they get an accurate, truthful view of problems and situations. They are more focused, proactive, and creative with their solutions, because they know what the problems are as they occur. And they have all the information they need to respond quickly and effectively.

In addition, honest communication allows organizations to attract and retain talented people, because those people feel as if they can succeed in such an honest and healthy environment. In this environment, people listen to and trust each other. They exchange valuable feedback so that goals are achieved and organizations are properly positioned to seize opportunities.

How are you and your organization advancing in the area of honest communication? Do you think there may be some areas that need improvement? Is a storm brewing? To see if you might have some hidden problems with honesty, please answer these Eleven Key Questions to Detect an Honest Communication Problem. (Although this focuses on work issues, you can easily translate it to personal or home issues as well.) If you answer no to any of these questions, an honest communication problem that could threaten you and your organization may be looming.

1. **Do you always react positively when someone shares difficult information or unpopular opinions with you?**
   Many times we say we want honest communication, but when someone gives it to us, we become upset or defensive. We may respond with a nasty look, a raised voice, or by ignoring what has been said. These types of responses speak volumes to the messenger and discourage this person from sharing difficult information or unpopular opinions in the future. In essence, a negative response trains and conditions people not to be forthcoming. If this continues, we might one day say, "Why am I the last one to know? Why didn't

anyone tell me?" The key is to own up to the situation and create a safe environment. Then people can say what needs to be said.

2. **Are you the first to hear and find out about things?**
   People who are afraid to say things directly to you often tell others in the organization what they truly think and feel. Unfortunately, when you finally hear this information indirectly, it is often severely distorted. Remember the game of telephone? Do you remember how distorted the message became after it had passed through several players? Distorted information thwarts our actions, because it is inaccurate. I have watched many projects and contracts become problematic, because they were built and executed based on hearsay information. Being the first to hear and directly find out facts is the key to handling things efficiently and effectively. That is why some of the best executives and managers develop ways to receive direct communication from their customers, potential customers, and all levels of their staff.

3. **Do people tell you everything you need to know?**
   How many times have you finished a project or made a decision only to find out that people did not share key information and ideas that would have altered or changed what you did? You may have thought, *If they had just said something, I might have taken care of this issue more effectively and in a fraction of the time.* Key information is often there — we just need to receive it. Honest and open communication is *crucial* to getting a quality job done on time, within budget.

4. **Do people argue, debate, and share opposing opinions in your presence?**

   President Lyndon Johnson said, "If nobody is arguing, only one person is thinking." I would add, "or only one person is being honest." It is normal and healthy to have differing opinions; the key is whether people have the freedom to share those differing opinions, tough news, and other information. If people around you never oppose your ideas and plans, they may not be saying what they are really thinking. If everyone always agrees with you, they probably do not. One reason for this dynamic is that people often suffer from The Authority Pleasing Principle — telling their leaders what they think they want to hear. Many people have been conditioned that the way to make people happy and advance in life is to do just that. Think about how our schooling may have conditioned us in that way. If we gave the teacher what he or she wanted, we were rewarded. In addition to the desire to please, employees often fear potential backlash if they share unpopular points of view. When we try to move forward and make a decision, we find that others are dragging their feet and not doing what we need them to do. In other words, they have not bought into the idea. We need to create a safe environment so people can say what they are really thinking — because receiving difficult information and feedback is essential to taking care of problems before they become huge issues.

5. **Do people keep their promises to you?**

   People who blatantly break their promises may be breaking other promises we are unaware of. As the saying goes, "Where there is smoke, there is fire." Watch out for those who say they may not keep their word on *small* stuff but will keep their word on the *big* stuff. This is usually not the case. People who do not keep their promises or who constantly adjust their promises and still don't deliver are probably not being upfront about something. Sometimes they know inside that they can't deliver, but they are afraid of our reaction or they don't want to let us down. Others feel weak or defeated when they admit they can't accomplish something. So, they are not truthful and upfront about what is really going on. Of course, the failure to come clean only compounds the problem, and in the end everyone pays a severe price. So an undelivered promise is often a symptom of a problem than needs to be discussed and resolved.

6. **Can you ask the questions that need to be asked?**
   People who have something to hide often don't react well when questions are asked. By getting defensive and having a strong reaction, a person can create an environment in which others back off because they are afraid to ask questions. This enables the hiding to continue. On the flip side, we have to recognize our contribution to the problem and our history of asking questions. For example, have you asked the person questions and then used the information later to punish them — even inadvertently? If so, this may explain why the person is defensive or guarded. So if you are uneasy about asking questions, this might be an indication to further examine the situation.

7. **When you ask a question, do people answer it directly?**
   People who are hiding things often skirt the issue, change the subject, or answer questions in global, ambiguous, or vague ways. Often they gloss over the present situation and jump to the future. In fact, some people not only don't

answer the question, they turn it around and ask you a question that distracts you. This tactic often works. For example, if you ask someone about the status of a report, they may say, "Fine. Just working hard. So, what do you have going on for the rest of the week?" How often have you walked away from discussions thinking, *I don't think they ever answered my question.* Further and persistent questioning is often the key to discovering and eventually resolving the problem.

8. Do people tell you consistent things?

If you listen closely to what someone says and they are not being upfront, you will often notice inconsistencies. Not being upfront takes energy, a great memory, and lots of creative stories. Most people are unable to maintain this over time. Their inconsistencies should spur you to probe further.

9. Do the people around you display a range of emotions?

People who only show one emotion are often not telling us everything. Displaying a range of emotions is natural and normal. Have you ever had someone, like a co-worker, client, or a friend, always tell you how great things are or how wonderful you are? Although this might be nice to hear and believe, the reality is that no one is always happy and, in particular, always happy with us. We have all heard stories about someone who thought others were happy only to later discover the real truth — their co-worker was not pleased with their work, the contract was not renewed, their spouse filed for separation, or their child was having major problems in school. So seeing and hearing only one emotion from someone can be a sign of a problem that should be further explored.

10. **Do people associate with others who you know to be upfront and honest?**

    By looking at who people surround themselves with, we can get an indication of the kind of person they truly are. The old saying, "Birds of a feather flock together," is true. People tend to surround themselves with those who are similar. If someone who claims to be trustworthy is constantly in the company of those who are not, it begs the question: why would they choose to be around people who do not share the same values? There may be a good explanation — the associates may be relatives or long-time friends who have been there during tough times. At the very least, however, someone's odd or questionable associates should cause you to be extremely cautious until you can fully understand the situation.

11. **Are people sharing innovative and even crazy ideas and opportunities with you?**

    In today's incredibly competitive work world, we must tap into the resources, ideas, and knowledge of the people around us. Research indicates that many of the greatest ideas do not come from headquarters but the front lines. Staff on the front lines are the closest to the problems, issues, and challenges. They know the way things *really* work. Without front-line information, feedback, and perspective, an organization can become stale, lose its competitive edge, and ultimately become extinct. This is why we need to constantly ask people for their ideas. Honest communication is not only essential to resolving issues but also in exploring new ideas and opportunities.

If these questions have exposed some problems in your organization or your personal relationships, you are now aware of the situation and can do something about it. Many individuals and organizations don't ask the hard questions quickly enough to uncover problems before the damage is done. Many people believe it is better not to rock the boat. They just hope things will get better. Maybe it is time to rock the boat and find out what may be lurking below so that you don't pay an even heavier price later.

Here are three suggestions that can have an immediate impact.

1. Organizations, no matter the size, must take specific and tangible actions to create a safe environment for employees to openly and honestly communicate.

2. Leaders must set the tone and the example by consistently demonstrating honest communication and being open to receive honest communication. They must show that it can be done, is appreciated, and will be rewarded.

3. Employees need to have or need to be taught the skills and techniques to communicate honestly and effectively. People talk about being honest, but few are actually shown *how* to do it and produce the desired results. These skills will enable employees to effectively express concerns about thorny or complicated issues without fear of a strong reaction from the receiver.

By approaching this on several levels and from different angles, an honest communication environment can flourish and thrive. This way, people can say what they need to say and find out what they need to find out. Ideas can be freely and safely exchanged, and everyone benefits. One easy, first step is to share the "Eleven Key

Questions to Detect an Honest Communication Problem" as a point of conversation.

If you detect honest communication problems, then iron out a plan to make a significant difference in the level of honest communication. Take action before it is too late!

10 Tips to Immediately Improve Your Life!

I TRUST YOU now have some great ideas, insights, strategies, techniques, tips, and tools that will have an immediate impact on your work and home life. These solutions can put your life on a different path. It's like flipping the switch on a train track — the initial change is minimal, but down the line the difference can be enormous. Honesty can be the switch that moves the train to a different track and the fuel that continues to move the train wherever you want it to go.

A change for the good in one area can have a positive effect on other areas and relationships as well. Throughout this book, we've discussed that the only person you can control is *you*. We challenge and support you to hold yourself accountable, take action, be your best, and be the best to others. You deserve to live your life this way.

The key is to take action to get what you want. The following ten actions can immediately improve the quality of your life.

In fact, I am so confident that these suggestions will positively affect the quality of your life, that I would like you to send me an e-mail (honest@StevenGaffney.com) detailing what you did and your results. If you do that, I will send you our new perpetual calendar that can be used year after year. The calendar also makes a great gift! I am committed to helping people get the results they want. I want to encourage you to take action — and I love to hear about your successes. You might even find your story in a future book.

Here are the ten actions to take that will make an immediate improvement.

1. **Find out if your "clients" are happy.**
   Remember that your clients are not only your customers but also your boss, your co-workers, your family, and your friends. Knowing what it takes to make them happy will make your life easier. Choose your most difficult "client" — the one you would like to improve things with — and ask, "On a scale of 1 to 10, how would you rate our relationship/this project/my effectiveness in this job/etc.?" Wait for their answer. Then ask, "What would it take to make it a 10?" Then for extra credit, ask, "What would it take to make it a 15 — above and beyond expectations?" Be ready for an interesting and — hopefully — helpful response.

2. **Call someone you've had a major issue with.**
   Resolve it, forgive them, agree to disagree… whatever the case, do what it takes to reach some sort of resolution or put it behind you. You could ask, "What would it take for us to put this behind us?" Extending the olive branch can create a

new beginning, triggering other conversations and events that can ultimately change your life.

3. **Have a conversation with someone you have a small issue with.**

    Address and resolve a small issue now before it becomes a BIG issue. Someone once said, "Problems are not like wine; they don't get better over time." Let the person know that you care about them and you do not want the issue to grow. Ask, "How would you suggest we specifically resolve this?" Their input can help you create a solution that works for everyone.

4. **Acknowledge someone you care about.**

    Send that person a thoughtful card inscribed with a list of what you've learned from them. All of us want to know that we make a difference. Let that special person know what a difference they make in your life. Tell them why and watch the joy you bring to them.

5. **Seek the counsel of at least three people who are older and wiser than you are.**

    Ask these people what important lessons they have learned in their lives. Sit still and listen. They can share secrets and insights that only time, experience, and wisdom can provide.

6. **Teach someone in your life a strategy, technique, or tip you learned from this book.**

    Teach them something that really made a difference for you. Teaching helps us re-learn and remember a strategy as well as positively impact someone else's life. Here's a helpful hint:

consider teaching a strategy to someone that might make YOUR life a little easier.

7. **Interview someone who is important to you and ask what his or her top priorities are for the year.**
   This knowledge will help you have a better relationship with them, because you will know where they are headed and how they view things.

8. **Commit to changing a behavior and being accountable in a public way.**
   For example, if you find yourself complaining about a particular issue and you want to stop being so negative, tell five people you are going to stop complaining about the issue. Every time you complain about the issue, give them each a dollar. This sends a message that you are really committed. Accountability is often the key to making lasting changes.

9. **Reach out to someone you have written off or given up on.**
   Stubbornness can get in the way of relationships, and regrets can plague us for the rest of our lives. Don't live with regret or doubt. Don't wait, seize the moment!

10. **Decide on your number-one goal and create a plan to achieve it.**
    Make sure your goal is measurable and that there is a deadline for completion. Remember that time is the one commodity we can never replenish when it is gone. Make sure you spend time achieving what you really want to achieve.

You can accomplish these ten actions if you are committed to changing your life. What if I were going to give you a billion dollars to take these actions? What if your life depended on them? If you really want to achieve this, you will. Take advantage of the promise I made to you at the beginning of this final chapter and let me know your results. I am in your corner, and together we can make a difference.

About the Author

HIGH-PROFILE CORPORATE consultant Steven Gaffney subscribes to the old adage: "Honest is the best policy." He'll be quick to note that he doesn't claim any moral high ground, acknowledging that he's as human as anyone. He just knows that honesty works.

As one of the foremost authorities on honest, open communication in the workplace, Steven Gaffney is on a self-described *crusade* for effective communication and has become the go-to guy for organizations across America. He provides the "Honesty Edge" that helps organizations gain a competitive advantage by resolving issues through open, honest communication.

In fact, thousands of people credit Steven Gaffney's keynote speeches, short sessions, intense multi-day seminars, his media appearances, and book *(Just Be Honest: Authentic Communication Strategies That Get Results and Last a Lifetime)* in making a critical difference in their lives and careers. Through his celebrated speeches, seminars, and books in the area of honest communication, Steven Gaffney offers an effective and tangible approach to resolving communication problems in the workplace.

The Steven Gaffney Company's clients include: Marriott, SAIC, BP, the Navy, NASA, the Food and Drug Administration, the Environmental Protection Agency, the Department of Commerce, American Express, Texas Instruments, and the American Cancer Society, to name a few. Serving such a diverse clientele has enabled Steven to create and implement innovative, cross-disciplined solutions.

Interesting Note: When you hear Steven speak, you might immediately think he is a natural and gifted orator. This was not always the case. By the age of three, Steven mumbled only a few words, and a doctor advised his mother that he should be put in special classes for slow children. Steven's mother did not accept this, and doctors eventually discovered that Steven's inability to speak was caused by multiple ear infections. After several operations, those problems were corrected, but Steven was delayed in learning how to communicate. His mother took him to Easter Seals for speech therapy, where they successfully taught Steven to speak. No one has been able to silence him since.

Contacting Us

Visit www.StevenGaffney.com to learn more about the Steven Gaffney Company, including our other products and services. Be sure to check out our life-changing honest communication seminar entitled, "The Fish Isn't Sick... The Water's Dirty." Our site contains a lot of FREE and helpful information. Also, you can call us at 703-241-7796 or toll free at 877-6-HONEST (877-646-6378) to receive more information.

Please let us know your results! If you e-mail us at Honest@StevenGaffney.com with a success story and we use it, we'll send you a free gift! You will also be entered in a drawing to receive a year's worth of private coaching from the Steven Gaffney Company.

Together we can make a difference!

Receiving Our Free Bi-Weekly Columns

IF YOU ENJOYED this book, sign up for Steven Gaffney's FREE bi-weekly e-mail advice on communication, motivation, and leadership. This book is based on previous advice columns. The Steven Gaffney Company is always developing more strategies, techniques, and tips. Visit www.stevengaffney.com to sign up and view other archived advice columns.

Ordering Information

JMG Publishing books are available online and at your favorite bookstores.

Quantity discounts are available to qualifying institutions.

All JMG Publishing books are available to the booktrade and educators through all major wholesalers.

For more information, call toll-free 877-6-HONEST.